FLASH! SPLASH! CRASH!

FLASH! SPLASH! CRASH!

ALL AT SEA WITH CAP'N BOB

My astonishing adventures with
ROBERT MAXWELL

MIKE MALONEY
and WILLIAM HALL

MAINSTREAM
PUBLISHING

EDINBURGH AND LONDON

First published in Great Britain in 1996 by
MAINSTREAM PUBLISHING COMPANY (EDINBURGH) LTD
7 Albany Street
Edinburgh EH1 3UG

ISBN 1 85158 853 1

A catalogue record for this book is available from the British Library

Typeset in Palatino
Printed and bound in Great Britain by Butler and Tanner Ltd, Frome

'I don't go in for ego trips. It's not my style.'

Robert Maxwell, explaining why he renamed his company
Maxwell Communications Corporation, September 1987.

'Are you ready, Mr Snapper?'

Robert Maxwell, waiting in line to be presented to
President Mikhail Gorbachev, to Mike Maloney, June 1990.

CONTENTS

Before

Why me?

Well, why not? Someone had to do it. But why, out of all the photographers that Cap'n Bob could have summoned across the seven seas of his enormous empire, did the century's most notorious privateer cast his eye on me and grant me the dubious halo of appointing me his personal photographer?

It would last for seven bizarre, unforgettable years, and at the end of it I was a changed man. Not necessarily for the better, but most definitely changed.

The truth is that under Robert Maxwell's stewardship, the oceans of the world opened out to show me undreamed-of horizons. I'm talking about a sea awash with caviar, champagne and the high life – after which, there's no going back. I mean, how do you come to terms with the real world after spending seven years spinning round the globe in private jets, pressing the flesh with royalty and presidents, when money is no object, and there are little extras like signing the odd hotel bill for almost £60,000 for a five-day stay? You tell me.

But why me? One answer, so I have been told more than once, is that R.M. – one of many titles we called him, depending on his mood or the moment – looked on me as a surrogate son following the death of his beloved first-born boy on a life-support machine in the Churchill Hospital, Oxford.

That young man, heir to the Maxwell fortunes, had been in a coma for five years, poor kid, following a crash when a car in which he was a passenger rammed the rear of a lorry outside the city when he was on the way home from a dance. The date was 27 January 1968. He was 21, tall and dark-haired – just like me. Had he recovered, he would have been only two years older than I was when I first met his father in 1984. And his name was Michael. His father loved him with the fierce, often almost frightening passion and possessiveness which he bestowed on anything or anyone he really cared for. He kept his son alive for five long years, refusing to give up hope, visiting him every day when he could.

So who knows? I don't, and I can only guess.

What I do know is that from day one of my first tremulous meeting with this formidable mountain of a man I was treated as one of the family. Eventually I came to look on Cap'n Bob, who managed the remarkable feat of being both respected and reviled as he stalked the pavements of Fleet Street, almost as a father figure . And, believe it or not, someone for whom I could even feel a certain genuine affection. But, okay, I could also tell a seasoned rogue when I saw one.

CHAPTER ONE

Early Days

My first encounter with Robert Maxwell was a brief one. All that was missing was Rachmaninov's *Fifth*.

It was 10.15 a.m. on the morning of Monday, 16 July 1984, and the *Daily Mirror* had acquired a new publisher (or vice versa).

I had been summoned unexpectedly to the Ninth Floor of the *Mirror* Building in Holborn Circus to meet the great man himself. Why, I had no idea. Five minutes earlier, as the *Mirror*'s junior photographer, I had been sitting in my usual place at the down-table end of the Picture Desk six floors below wondering how the day would take shape. Now, in an outer office which was a beehive of activity with assistants and secretaries buzzing hither and thither, I was waiting for an audience with the new eminence in our midst.

I listened to advice from the accolytes, who seemed to know. 'Call him R.M. when you want to be formal, and when other people are in the room. Call him Publisher when the other people in the room are VIPs or when he is in a bad mood.'

'How will I know when he's in a bad mood?'

'Oh, you'll know!'

'Call him Boss. Or Chief. Or Chairman. He likes all of those. On a good day, with care, you may eventually be allowed to call him Bob.'

Playing safe to begin with, because I knew no better, I decided to call him 'Sir'.

The *Mirror* was still in a state of shock. Like everyone else on the Editorial floor, I had felt the tension crackling like static electricity around the vast room with its computers and screens lying oddly silent while we came to terms with a force ten gale about to blow through the entire building.

With the skill of a born predator, Maxwell had bullied and cajoled his way into achieving his great dream: buying up the *Daily Mirror* and all the other papers that went with it in a package worth millions.

Unknown to me, the new Chairman had arrived at the company's underground car park off Fetter Lane on that wet Monday morning sitting in the back of his maroon Silver Shadow Rolls-Royce. In front of him was his trusted chauffeur (and occasional bodyguard) Les Williams. Alongside him sat the *Mirror*'s Chief Executive, Douglas Long.

In fact, it wasn't the Boss's first visit to his new empire. The previous Friday, ominously the thirteenth, he had secretly driven to what would become known as the *Daily Maxwell* to view his great coup at first hand. When the security guard behind the desk in reception challenged him and inquired his business in the building, R.M. told him jovially: 'I've just bought it!' To which there really is no reply.

Now the limousine nosed past the barrier and searched for a bay. There was one space left.

By chance it happened to be next to a gleaming green and white Silver Shadow Rolls-Royce already parked there, complete with the personalised number plate 914 MM emblazoned on it.

My number plate. My Roller.

The Chairman stepped out, and surveyed my car in silence for a full minute. He noted that my Rolls was a year newer than his.

At last he asked heavily: 'Which one of my executives drives a Rolls-Royce, Douglas?'

'Er – it's not one of your executives, Chairman. It's the *Mirror*'s junior photographer.'

'Umm,' said Maxwell. Another thoughtful pause. Then, 'You'd better send this boy up to me. I want to meet him.'

Ten minutes later I was summoned to the Ninth Floor.

I had been with the paper some time, anxious to make my mark, and was still clawing my way up the lower rungs. Lower rungs can be slippery – but then, aren't they all?

Now there I was in the leather-walled executive lift, straightening my tie, heading upwards – to what? It was the first time I had ever set foot at this rarefied height. If it wasn't altitude sickness, I was certainly feeling a trifle queasy with a mixture of apprehension and curiosity.

Part of me couldn't wait to meet the new Boss. The other part wasn't so sure. His reputation had preceded him. The man once described as Czechoslovakia's second most explosive export after Semtex had been desperate to buy himself a newspaper empire. He made his first bid for a Fleet Street national in 1968, spreading an exploratory tentacle out for the *News of the World*. Rupert

Bob blowing his own trumpet after taking over Mirror Group Newspapers.

Murdoch foiled him. In 1981 he had tried again, this time for the *Sun* and *The Times*. Again Murdoch beat him to the punch.

Never one to give up easily – in fact never one to give up, period – Maxwell staked a claim on both the Express Group and the *Sunday Times*, and came up empty-handed. That same year, 1984, he had failed to buy *The Observer* from Lonrho and Tiny Rowland.

The war of attrition he would fight with Rupert Murdoch – the 'Dirty Digger', as lampooned in satirical magazines – would be written into Grub Street legend. In fact they had first met in Sydney in the late '60s, when Rupert invited Robert home to play poker, after which Maxwell would proudly recall: 'I won!'.

It was the only game he would win against the Aussie tycoon who, three times, snatched newspapers from under his nose.

But at last, having played the field in Fleet Street for so long, Maxwell came up trumps. He knew that the publishing giant Reed International planned to

Being photographed by a television company with my Rolls-Royce.

float the Mirror Group on the stock market rather than sell it to an individual. But the going market price was only around £60 million. The inveterate dawn raider pounced, and proposed £113 million, an offer they couldn't refuse.

But why newspapers, when his huge company BPCC (British Printing and Communication Corporation) – which he called 'my war horse' – was worth £1 billion?

'Publishing a national newspaper is one way of reminding a country it can fight back,' was one memorable utterance from the Boss to explain his obsession, magnificent or otherwise.

More to the point was something I heard from John Pilger, the investigative journalist and a former *Mirror* man himself. 'Prime ministers seldom come to lunch with someone who prints labels on cans of baked beans, however many labels they print or however rich it has made them,' he said. 'But prime ministers do come to lunch with the publishers of national papers – including the *Daily Mirror* . . . ' How true.

So there I was, poised outside the heavy polished mahogany door with the word PRIVATE scrolled on it. Five . . . ten . . . 15 minutes, during which time I examined my fingernails and managed to refrain from biting them.

All around, there was a hum of activity.

Finally the squawk-box crackled on the desk of the Chairman's personal assistant, Debbie Dines, and I heard a deep voice 'Send in Mr Maloney!'

I knocked on the heavy door with timid knuckles, and passed through into the inner sanctum.

'Ah!'

My first impression was of a vast mahogany desk that seemed to take up the whole of the far end of the room. Behind it, an equally vast figure was surveying me.

My second impression: eyebrows. Two of them, plastered like twin black limpets on a massive forehead above a dark, forbidding gaze.

Odd, because a lot of people would say the same thing to me in the months to come when they first met Robert Maxwell. 'Eyebrows.' Odd, but true.

My image widened like a camera in reverse zoom to reveal a bear-like figure built like a barrage balloon, in shirt-sleeves. His dark-blue jacket hung over his chair. A refreshingly colourful tie in jaunty red and yellow stripes relieved any possible hint of sombreness.

Later we would hear that at the first editorial meeting, which in fact had already taken place over the weekend, Maxwell insisted that all the executives present removed their jackets and that they would continue to do so at all future meetings.

For now, my immediate sense was that I was about to be eaten for

Lieutenant Robert Maxwell, war hero.

breakfast. PUBLISHER SWALLOWS PHOTOGRAPHER WHOLE. Nice headline.

My new boss surveyed me with an unnerving stare and did not invite me to sit down. It was like looking down the twin barrels of a shotgun, and knowing the gun is loaded.

His opening words were not encouraging, either.

'Do I pay you too much, Mister?'

I would learn later that the Chairman always called people Mister when he was displeased.

With the courage of youth, I piped up: 'No, you certainly don't, Mr Maxwell.'

'Then how come you can afford to drive a Rolls-Royce?'

Good question. I searched for a good answer to match it.

The truth was that I had bought my Rolls second-hand, after months of saving. I had always hungered for a Rolls-Royce, albeit a second-hand one, and finally I found one at a price that wouldn't have me begging on the streets to pay for it.

I tilted my jaw defiantly and looked him straight in the eye. 'I work very hard. I earn my money.'

Rash perhaps, in hindsight. But a lot of my salary had gone into that car, and it was my pride and joy. Unexpectedly, the Great Bear in his new firmament seemed to like it, and without another word waved a large paw in dismissal.

Next day I became his personal photographer. This, you understand, was in addition to my regular duties, except that every time the Ninth Floor called I dropped everything, and ran.

What did I know of my new boss?

Frankly, not a lot.

I knew he was a one-time Labour MP and that he had been born in Czechoslovakia and was thus referred to as the 'Bouncing Czech' by *Private Eye* and sundry other organs, vital or otherwise. I knew that he had distinguished himself in World War II with an act of bravery that won him the Military Cross. As a Lieutenant in the North Staffordshire Regiment, it seems that virtually single-handed he routed an enemy squad holed up in a house in a fire-fight at Paarlo in January 1945. The 20-year-old officer led two of his sections through a hail of bullets to rescue some of our boys trapped in another building. The official citation included the words: *Showing no regard for his own safety . . . magnificent example and offensive spirit . . . this officer was responsible for the relief of the platoon . . .*

Field Marshal Montgomery himself presented the newly promoted Captain Robert Maxwell with his MC in March that year, and sent young Bob a photograph of the occasion to commemorate it.

During the Cold War that followed, Maxwell was suspected of being a double-agent with our chaps and the Russians, although the details ended up lost in a fog of uncertainty.

I had read of his various business dealings through a company he headed called Pergamon Press. Apart from that, I knew nothing.

I have to say that at that point I wasn't particularly interested, either. But if you're about to become the boss's personal lensman, it is advisable to obey the old boy-scout maxim: *Be Prepared*.

So I went to the *Mirror* library and searched the files. I found that Ian Robert Maxwell was born Ludvik Hoch on 10 June 1923, eldest son of a poverty-stricken Czech labourer, and grew up in the village of Solotvino in the Carpathian Mountains. The family – three sons, six daughters – lived on Synagogue Street in the centre of the village.

At the age of six, little Ludvik contracted diphtheria, and survived because his mother swapped her only pillow for a sledge to rush her son through the snows to hospital in the middle of the night.

He built a successful publishing business, specialising in scientific books and journals, which made him a millionaire. In 1964 he became the Labour MP for Buckingham, holding the seat until 1970. He had made increasingly desperate efforts to become a newspaper baron.

But now Cap'n Bob, as the cartoon strip in *Private Eye* dubbed him, had hit the jackpot and was flying high. As it turned out, rather like Icarus. As for me, I got caught in the slipstream.

My first assignment gave me a hint of the shape of things to come.

Being the Big Man's personal photographer could become a major headache. Not just for me, but for the *Daily Mirror* Picture Desk. One phone call from the Ninth Floor – and everything else had to be dropped. It meant that photo sessions I had worked on for weeks would be shelved at the last minute, causing havoc, bad feeling and muttering in the ranks.

I could have spent hours on the phone persuading a model or an actress to pose for us in the studio, only to have to make my excuses and leave it to some other lucky lensman to do the honours.

It was useless to protest and when the call came from 'On High', I jumped. The only question, as some wag put it, was, *How high?*

The call came. It was from shapely Debbie, complete with her dark hair, voluptuous figure and Aussie accent – Maxwell always did have an eye for a pretty girl.

'The Chairman is entertaining Senator John Tower to lunch. He wants you to

With Senator John Tower – who was soon to witness an unsightly incident on the roof.

photograph them together on the roof when the Senator leaves for Heathrow. Would you please stand by at two o'clock.'

For 'would you', read *Be There!*

Leaving from the roof meant the Maxwell helicopter waiting patiently for its master on the astro-turf helipad that adorned the heights of Maxwell House, next to the *Mirror* building, and which brought a splash of green to the drab grey rooftops of Holborn. Which, in turn, meant the guest was getting VIP treatment.

I had never heard of Senator John Tower – he could have been Senator John Doe as far as I was concerned. A quick call to the Ninth Floor, however, elicited the information that Senator Tower had indeed made a special trip from Washington by Concorde for a business meeting with the Chairman. He was due to take the evening Concorde home again on a quick turnaround.

Senator Tower was former chairman of the Senate Armed Forces Committee, and had now been appointed chairman of Pergamon Brassey, the defence publishing arm of Bob's BPCC Publishing Corporation.

In a message to *Mirror* staff in our house magazine *Progress*, the senator had given a eulogistic homily extolling the virtues of the firm.

'I am bound to say that this company makes an invaluable contribution to the defence of the free world. I am very pleased to be working with Robert Maxwell and Kevin Maxwell because the company enjoys a high reputation in the governments and defence departments around the world for the accuracy and creativity of their pubications.'

Well, we all felt better for that.

I made my way to the roof of Maxwell house, where the outline of the helicopter squatted on its orange painted cross like a giant gnat, complete with its growling lion logo and the *Mirror* insignia FORWARD WITH THE PEOPLE plastered on its side.

The wind sock hung limply on its stand.

There was rain in the air, and a few spots fell as I checked my camera while I waited.

There was no sign of the boss, or his guest. Another 30 minutes elapsed, as the rain spattered thick drops on the green artificial turf. I introduced myself to the Captain, Dick Cowley, and we chatted desultorily, keeping a weather eye open for the Very Important Passenger.

Finally the steel door to the stairwell scraped open. Maxwell and a middle-aged, middle-sized, jovial figure emerged, both of them wearing that look of mutual *bonhomie* that successful businessmen sport after a successful business lunch.

Senator Tower might have passed for a football coach if you'd met him in the street. Indeed, the boss would tell me later that they had spent most of the time talking soccer, discussing the difference between English and American football, along with a few more important financial matters that he was not prepared to disclose.

Maxwell had just entered a whole new ball game by purchasing Oxford United FC, and would soon be bidding for Derby County. His sights were set on becoming a big wheel in our national game.

Cap'n Bob with his personal helicopter, call sign VR-BOB (for 'Very Rich Bob') on the roof of Maxwell House.

Meantime, I rattled off some shots of them together by the helicopter. Weeks later, I would find myself photographing them again, in dinner jackets, after a formal dinner in Washington.

But for now . . . 'This way, Publisher! And you, Senator. Would you care to shake hands . . . ?'.

I was about to pose them against another background when, without warning, my Chairman suddenly reached down to his trousers, undid his zip and called out heartily: 'Hey, Senator, how about taking a leak before you get into the chopper!

With which cordial invitation he pulled out his best friend, strode over to the parapet, and proceeded to piddle from a great height on to the lunch-time crowds bustling along New Fetter Lane ten floors below.

I can still see the look on John Tower's face.

'But Bob! *Bob!* What about the people below?' he exclaimed.

'Don't worry about them,' Mr Subtlety shouted back reassuringly, still clutching his member. 'By the time the piss hits them, they'll think it's drizzle!'

That was one exposure I didn't take.

The Senator scrambled hastily into the helicopter without taking advantage of his host's invitation.

This time he didn't even stop to shake hands.

Big Bob began his march to glory. At least, that was the way he saw it.

In direct contrast to the Duke of Wellington, and the effect his men had on him – 'By God, they terrify me!' – I was able to witness at first-hand how Cap'n Bob put the fear of God (and Maxwell) into his own troops.

When he strode into Maxwell House, he walked into an organisation that has since been variously described as 'a snake-pit of slackness, decay and corruption'. These were the days when the all-powerful printing unions ran the shop.

It has been written into Fleet Street folklore how printers clocked in as M. Mouse, D. Duck and even James Bond to pick up overtime under second aliases, and how some were so drunk on a Friday night that they couldn't remember their own pseudonyms when they staggered in from the White Hart pub in New Fetter Lane, affectionately known as the 'Stab in the Back'.

Maxwell was aware of how Roy Thomson, the tycoon who ran Thomson Newspapers, had walked the hot coals of union contempt when he acquired the *Sunday Times* in 1959. Another tale of legend was that Thomson, a shrewd Canadian, had chosen the softly-softly approach when visiting his new baby. In the machine room, he said to a printer: 'I'm Roy Thomson, the new owner of the paper.'

To which came the bleak and decidedly unhelpful reply: 'You may own it. But we run it.'

The new kid on the block would have none of such mutiny. Cap'n Bob led with the prow of his chin, and combining a Machiavellian mix of affability and ruthlessness he brought the unions into line. It was either that, he told them, or walk the plank. He would close everything down, sink the ship – and that meant all hands with it. As he told Joe Haines, his Political Editor and one of his several biographers: 'The gravy train has hit the buffers!'. . .

Two years later, I would learn that over the months my new boss had engineered or overseen the sacking of 8,000 employees in his myriad companies. Now there's style for you.

The Chairman's sumptuous living-room at Maxwell House.

Personally, I was more concerned about not becoming victim number 8,001. So I was intrigued to learn what one of his former editors, an equally charismatic character named Robert Edwards, famous for his snow-white hair and permanent tan, had to say about his own ring-side seat at the 1984 blood-letting – er, that is take-over.

'Working for Maxwell,' he recalled, 'I found people tended to look at you as if you were a street accident victim. "What's he like?" they would ask. "It must be awful!" '.

Not for me, it wasn't. And as for that gravy train, it was only just steaming out of the station. Almost without realising it, I was sucked into the inner circle of the Maxwell fiefdom. But I had to prove myself – with my camera.

Early assignments consisted of my being first, available, and second, fast on my feet.

I became a regular visitor to the Ninth Floor, and was happy to take advice

High fliers in the Maxwell team: (left to right)Kevin Maxwell, R.M. Reg Mogg (finance), Richard Baker (Deputy Managing Director, MCC), Ron Woods (Director of Pergamon Holdings), John-Pierre Anselmini (Deputy Chairman, MCC).

from those in the know. Particularly helpful was Jean Baddeley, the Boss's personal assistant for more than 15 years, who could read the Cap'n like a book, and always seemed to be several pages ahead. To me, she was the consummate professional.

Jean was a slim, attractive woman who was totally trusted by Maxwell, and in all the years she was with him never betrayed that trust. For just reward, because he appreciated loyalty more than any other quality in his trusted lieutenants, he gave her a Porsche and eventually a directorship of Pergamon Holdings, his umbrella company.

On me, for starters, he bestowed the keys of the kingdom. Actually, a single key – the one that gave access to the Executive Lift for the use of the privileged few. This also meant access to his private luxury apartment on the Tenth Floor.

Jean gave me some opportune words of advice.

'Keep a bag packed at all times. And keep your passport handy. You're going to need it.'

'Tell me about yourself, Michael.' The Boss rose from behind his desk, and crossed to the fridge in the corner of his office. The room grew perceptibly smaller.

Cap'n Bob had that effect on people, and on his surroundings. Curiouser and curiouser, as Alice would have said, but they both seemed to shrink in his presence. He bent his unnerving stare on me. 'I presume you are not averse to champagne?'

'Certainly not, sir. I love it.'

I did, too. Particularly the Chairman's favourite – Dom Perignon, vintage '83.

He poured two glasses.

'Well?'

About myself? It was the first time that Robert Maxwell had shown any interest in his personal photographer whatsoever, and we were three months into his reign as El Supremo of Mirror Group Newspapers.

In that time, something quite remarkable had happened. People were buying the papers: the *Daily Mirror*, its sisters the *Sunday Mirror* and the *People*. And the one paper that could surely never fall at any fence – the bible of horse-racing, the *Sporting Life*. The graph was going up.

He gestured at an armchair. 'Sit down,' and he handed me a glass. We were alone for the first time in all those weeks. It was seven o'clock on a Friday night.

For the first time nobody was outside trying to break the door down to beat a path to his desk. The outside office was empty. Everyone had gone home.

Soon, of course, the first edition would be running, and the usual hell would be let loose as the Publisher started rattling cages. But for now, there was a brief oasis of tranquillity.

I told him about myself. How I was born in Lincoln. and was aged ten when my father bought me my first camera, a bakelite Kodak 127 which I still treasure to this day.

'You've still got it?' He sounded incredulous.

'Yes, it's in a drawer at home, and it still takes pictures.'

He bent a benevolent gaze on me. 'Does it?'

I told him about my first photographic assignment when I was 17, a greenhorn freelance for the local *Lincolnshire Chronicle* covering the annual Boy Scouts' Parade at Lincoln Cathedral.

He perked up. 'How much did they pay you?'

'The princely sum of ten shillings and sixpence.

'Umm. Hardly a small fortune.'

'Well, it was a start.'

My Rolls-Royce, with personalised number plate.

I was just getting into my stride, when he cut me short. 'I was the youngest photographer in Fleet Street, and – '

'Let me tell you what I have learned from my own start, Mike. Can you keep a secret?'

Lesson one. The Publisher has a low boredom threshold, unless he is talking about himself. Four glasses of DP, and his voice had sunk into a rumble, a volcano in pre-eruption.

I just sat there and listened.

'Well, yes, I – '

'A secret has to be between two people, not three. Do you know why, Michael?'

'Er – no, sir.'

He leaned forward on his elbows, and fixed me with an unwavering stare. His sonorous voice sank even deeper, almost out of hearing.

'You can always shoot the other person.'

Remembering how Lieutenant Bob won his MC, who was I to argue?

I felt he was warming to me.

How did I photograph the Boss to make him look good? First off, disguise his paunch. His beer belly – as some unkindly described it – expanded along with his wealth and success. The one thing that Bob liked about me was that I had this ability to make him look slim in photographs. How so?

There is a technique to this. It is the angle you employ, the lens you use, and the focal length that will actually elongate the subject in your shutter frame.

Believe me, it works. I can actually make anyone look heavier than they are – and, more important with Cap'n Bob, make them look slimmer.

I remember how I used to photograph somebody like Pat Rothermere, known as Bubbles to one and all, hostess to the world. She would surge into a room like a Spanish galleon – but by employing this technique I would be able to show her the prints next day, and she would say: 'Oh Mike, they're wonderful!'

Well, they weren't that wonderful. But they made Bubbles look a lot slimmer, which was all that mattered.

As for Cap'n Bob, his best angle was taken from above, looking down. And using a wide-angle lens to make him look taller and slimmer. Well, yes, I was sometimes tempted to set the lens the other way to make him look shorter and fatter. But then, I wasn't about to commit suicide.

One other thing I was careful *not* to do with my new Boss was to shoot him with the flash below the camera.

Why not? Because it gives a dreadful ghoulish effect, highlighting the wrong features and making the subject look like Dracula. So my tip has always been that when you have a camera with a built-in flash, and turn the camera for a vertical picture from horizontal, always make sure the flash is at the top of the camera and not at the base.

Simple, really. People don't think of those things. But as Cap'n Bob's new blue-eyed boy, I had to give such details serious consideration. My whole future depended on it.

CHAPTER TWO

Hey, Big Spender!

It was six p.m. on a Sunday evening and I was still trying to come to terms with my new job (as personal photographer to the Publisher) and my new status in this unexpected rise in my fortunes. Also, the fact that I was supposed to be at Cap'n Bob's beck and call 24 hours of the day and night.

In the lounge of my home in St Albans, Hertfordshire, I had settled down on the sofa with a cheese sandwich to watch television when the phone rang.

R.M. was on the line in person. Very rarely did he call me himself so I knew it must be important. What I didn't know was that he had been celebrating.

The heavy, familiar voice came across. 'Michael, are you busy?'

Not any more.

'I want you to chronicle the signing of a very important document. Now!'

I was in St Albans, he was in Holborn. With an inward sigh, I bade farewell to my cheese sandwich and headed the office BMW down the A1 and into Maxwell House within 40 minutes.

Using my personal blue security electronic pass key, which is shaped like a credit card, I took the Executive Lift to the Tenth Floor, and into the inner sanctum.

Inside his private office, Bob was in shirt-sleeves conducting a meeting – and he was in a very good mood. I could tell, because the first thing he pressed into my unresisting hand was a glass of Dom Perignon – in a half-pint tumbler!

The faithful few were gathered around, smiling, laughing: Peter Jay, chief of staff, Andrea Martin his personal PA, Number One Son Kevin, Simon Grigg the butler and Muriel, another girl assistant affectionately known as Mouse. The atmosphere was one of celebration and conviviality.

Bob was in one of the best moods I had ever seen. He was stroking a small wooden duck, caressing it like a kitten. Now where did that come from?

Celebrating! (left to right) Kevin Maxwell, 'Mouse', R.M., Simon Grigg, Andrea Martin, Peter Jay.

His first words to me were, 'You can understand, Michael, why I am calling you in tonight.'

No, Chief, I have no idea. But who am I to query it in this atmosphere of euphoria?

I sat down, nursing the tumbler. An hour went by, punctuated by a lot of laughter and joking. Obviously, something was in the wind.

It was apparent that he had pulled off some fabulous deal. I located my ever-present camera and shot off a few pictures of the occasion, not knowing why. Bob at his desk, with pen poised over a sheaf of documents. Bob raising a glass of champagne to his staff. Bob roaring with laughter.

'All right,' he said at last. 'We'll call that an evening.'

The others shuffled obediently towards the door. And went their separate ways with that look of concerted relief I had come to notice when people left the Chairman's private office sound in wind and limb, and with careers still intact.

I put my equipment away, and prepared to go home. Then Bob spoke again. 'I'm sorry I disturbed your Sunday evening, Mike, but you can now understand why this was so important.'

No, actually I couldn't, but I nodded vigorously.

'I'm glad it went well – er, Bob.' It was the first time I had ventured to step on that particular piece of uncharted turf.

He seemed to accept it. 'Have you eaten?'

No, I lied.

'Let's go and have some dinner.' He shrugged his huge bulk into his jacket. 'Come with me – and bring my briefcase.

'The briefcase was fashioned in elegant maroon leather, with a brass tag and the initals R.M. engraved on it. I picked it up from behind his desk and followed him out of the door. The others had gone, apart from Simon the butler who was clearing the bottles and glasses away.

We went down in the private lift and into the waiting Rolls-Royce. One of the reserve drivers was at the wheel, and the engine was running. As usual, Simon had tipped him off on the car phone that the Old Man was on his way down.

Off through Chancery Lane, then Holborn, and into the bright lights of the West End. I should have known better than to ask where we were going but I didn't, and I asked.

'You'll see,' was all he said.

I made a mental note, which was confirmed time and again in the months to come. Cap'n Bob sets the pace, and does the leading. You follow. Every conversation was like some curious dance – you had to anticipate, and try not to tread on his toes. Or, cardinal sin, step out of line with a careless remark that could be misinterpreted.

I was learning fast.

We ended up outside Maxims in Kensington, which I vaguely knew to be one of London's ultra-rich gambling clubs, strictly for the high rollers.

We were saluted in by a uniformed doorman, who I noticed jumped to the phone as Maxwell's large figure passed through. By the time we reached the restaurant, the maitre d' was waiting to bow us to the Boss's usual corner table.

I looked around, trying not to appear overwhelmed by the glittering chandeliers, candlelight, gleaming cutlery and bone china crockery.

I couldn't help noticing that most of the faces at the other tables were swarthier than ours. Some had groups of women only seated together in a variety of exquisite saris, kaftans and burkas. (These last, for the uninitiated, being the full-length robes worn by Muslim women in public that cover the whole of their body and head except the eyes.)

The reason I know this is because Bob told me. He saw me looking, and chuckled. 'Arabs, Indians, Koreans – that's where most of the big money comes from,' he said. 'Noisy lot, aren't they?'

They were, too. The chattering from the women sounded like a gaggle of hens. I noted that while they ate copiously, they only drank mineral water even as the liqueur trolley was wheeled past.

At least I didn't have that problem. Bob handed me the wine list. 'You choose it, Mike!'

'Are you sure, R.M.?'

'Yes. Go ahead. I want to see what you come up with.'

Nothing loth, I chose one of my all-time favourites – not a Chateau Margaux, as connoisseurs might expect, or even a Lafitte-Rothschild but a full-bodied Opus 1 from the Napa Valley in California. I played safe with a Chablis *Premier Cru* to go with the starters.

When the Opus arrived, Bob picked it up and studied it for a long minute. 'Amazing,' he said.

'What is, R.M.?'

'This is Betty's favourite. She prefers it to the Lafitte.' (Betty being Mrs Maxwell.)

Somehow I felt I had passed another test.

A flurry of waiters descended around us like a flock of homing pigeons. Bob ordered the food – lobster claws to start with, followed by belinis, lightly cooked caviar pancakes.

I couldn't help thinking of the half-eaten cheese sandwich still reposing by the sofa back home. I'd be missing *Songs of Praise* on the box, too. Ah well, you can't have everything.

Bob finished off his caviar, and drained the last glass of Opus 1. Then he said, 'Do you gamble, Mister?'

I shrugged. 'Well, I have been known to put a fiver on the Grand National. Each way.' In truth I never was much of a gaming man, figuring that life is enough of a gamble as it is.

But Bob was getting to his feet. 'Come with me! I will teach you how to play roulette. Bring my briefcase!'

His bulk lumbered ahead of me across the thick pile carpet and into the casino. In his wake, I suddenly recalled a story I had heard somewhere of his gambling methods – how he was rumoured to play three tables at a time. Impossible, surely? How can you sit between three tables, and make sense of the odds?

But he marched through the green baize tables as if he owned the place, to be greeted like royalty by fawning managers and croupiers. Maybe he *would* own it shortly, I thought, as he made for a roped-off corner area, strictly for high rollers only.

Or maybe he wouldn't.

The Boss settled his weight on to a gold-backed chair as if he intended to stay there. I perched myself on to one of the high stools just behind him, with a good view of the action. A dinner-jacketed croupier waited expectantly by the roulette wheel, and half a dozen other players, all male, all swarthy, stared at the new arrival with a mixture of interest and awe.

Without looking over his shoulder, Bob held up a hand. 'Give me some money, Michael!'

There was a brief but pregnant pause in the proceedings.

'Er – I haven't got any, R.M.,' I said lamely.

'From the briefcase, you fool!'

I flicked the lock. The briefcase sprang open. I stared down in disbelief.

Inside were wads of bank-notes in mint condition, each wrap freshly stamped. Closer, I could see they were in denominations of crisp 50s and 20s.

I handed him a bundle. There must have been £10,000 in that one. Bob threw it on the table, and in return received a veritable mountain of rectangular and circular chips from the croupier.

A rectangle, as far as I could work out, was worth £1,000. A circle meant £100. Bob's big hand pushed out chips across the green baize – on to single numbers. That meant odds of 36-to-one. And never a wimpish black or red, which at least would have been two-to-one.

'Watch for number 17, Mike – it's my lucky number,' he confided as the night wore on.

Bob with Betty . . .

It never came up.

The long night grew longer. The case on my lap grew perceptibly lighter.

I noticed Cap'n Bob's methods changing. I had no sense of panic from the mountainous figure hunched intently in front of me. But now he started to put his chips on quarters to reduce the odds.

One chip to cover four numbers.

Plus a £100 chip on lucky 17 with every rattle of that little ball-bearing in its tumble dryer on the wheel of fortune.

But in 90 minutes, never did a single number come up for him.

I fished around in the case. 'This is the last bundle, R.M.,' the paymaster bent to murmur in his ear. I suddenly felt like James Bond on a losing streak.

'Give it to me,' he ordered gruffly – and instead of playing the quarters, he went for all or nothing. Put the lot, all £10,000, on lucky 17.

And lost.

In those 90 minutes, Cap'n Bob had blown away £750,000.

. . . and with the boys: Ian left and Kevin.

'Oh well,' he said, and his brow was furrowed for the first time.'That's three quarters of a million gone.'

'Christ,' I thought.

My face must have given the game away. 'You look surprised, Mike! Don't worry – I've lost more than this before.' A pause. 'But I've won more than that before – and I'll do it again.'

He probably would. While I waited for the Chairman outside the cloakroom, a croupier confided in me that only the previous month my boss had won £1.5 million in a night, playing the same system.

So . . . you lose some, you win some.

We went back to Maxwell House in the Rolls. Bob extended a big paw. 'Goodnight Mike. Wasn't that fun? Thanks for coming. See you tomorrow!'

Feeling slightly shell-shocked, I headed back to St Albans. When I got home, I threw the curling cheese sandwich into the bin.

Dust and sand. Horrendous heat. Suddenly I am confronted with the Third World in all its awfulness at first hand, the world most of us are fortunate enough only to see on television from the comfort of our firesides.

My throat is constricted, I can't swallow properly – not through the heat but because of the dust hanging in the air. The effect is like swallowing hot marbles, and there is no escape from it.

It is October 1985, and I am on a humanitarian expedition with the Great Saviour from the Skies. Cap'n Bob, who else?

This is the famous *Mirror* Mercy Mission to save the poor and starving in the Sudan, with a chartered Jumbo 747 filled with tins of food and blankets to comfort that wretched famine-plagued country.

There are few things more bizarre than the empty interior of a 747 airliner, especially when it is flying at 35,000 feet. In the vastness of the first-class cabin, as big as your average hotel foyer, there are just three of us in the Maxwell team: Cap'n Bob and myself, with the Third Musketeer in the person of a *Mirror* reporter, Chris Gysin. We sit solemnly up front in our *Marie Celeste* of the skies, aware of our obligations to humanity, and also to the *Mirror*'s readership.

It was on this trip that I had my first experience of my new Boss's culinary etiquette. We were having chicken for lunch, somewhere over the Mediterranean.

I am in the seat immediately behind the chief when suddenly something comes whistling through the air at my head. I duck, and it sails harmlessly past my right ear.

A chicken leg! Or remains of same.

The chairman had tossed it casually over his shoulder for no reason I could begin to fathom. Another followed, heading across the aisle to smack against the window with a greasy squelch, followed by a third a few moments later.

'Flying chicken legs!' I muttered darkly to Chris in the next seat,' now I've seen everything.'

Cap'n Bob turned his attention to the newspapers. I could tell by the small wads of newsprint scrunched into balls and dropped carelessly at his feet. Soon there were enough to make the plane's interior look like a carpet of over -sized confetti.

A goodbye wave from Betty Maxwell.

This was another pattern I would see repeated time and again on my voyages with R.M.

Books, too. He would decimate them from page one tearing out pages and screwing them into a ball before tossing them on the floor. But, for now, it was just newspapers.

I was there to record the event for the pages of *the Daily Mirror*, and add another leaf to Maxwell's personal crown of laurels.

It was, of course, a circulation ploy designed to bolster the alarmingly shrinking figures of the paper. Things had changed After one year of Bob's reign, the *Mirror* was reported to have taken a massive 350,000 dive in sales, with an overall group loss near the one million mark. One trade paper had caustically remarked: 'It takes something close to genius to lose so much circulation so quickly.'

Personally, I was after the Big Picture. Let the Chairman enjoy his hour. I knew there would be something more lasting to give to the world outside that tragic land.

Sure enough, there was. We landed at Khartoum, with due publicity. Whereupon, after we checked in to our rooms, a waiting aide in the form of Neil Bentley, who had been despatched a week earlier, reported to the Boss with a problem.

'Chairman, I have to tell you that I can't use my toilet.'

'Why not?'

'Because it's blocked.'

'You're nothing but a big crapper,' the Chairman observed jovially.

Cap'n Bob's sense of humour was always, to put it kindly, somewhat basic. After which brilliant shaft of wit – or waft of you-know-what – poor Neil had to endure being known as the Big Crapper.

With his good deed done and duly recorded world-wide, Bob headed for home, a lone figure in an empty 747. I stayed on, with Chris Gysin – and with a job to do.

In my mind, I wanted to encapsulate and symbolise the dire situation of the starving thousands, struggling to stay alive in their shanty towns of makeshift tents with their babies dying in front of me. Above all, I wanted to capture the futility of it all. There must have been half a million of them, and I know we have seen equally harrowing sights since – but this was one image that lives with me to this day.

I found what I was looking for when I spotted a tiny baby, as small as a sparrow, its foot no bigger than a man's finger. It was six months old, not new-born – but about to die.

No bigger than a man's finger . . .

Getting accustomed to the high life.

Bob on his Mercy Mission to Africa.

That was the picture I took, a small black foot in the helpless hand of a white doctor. And that was the picture that appeared across half a page in the *Sunday Mirror* on 10 March 1985 – life-size, for impact.

When I finally returned home, the picture had been published. The Chairman called me up to his office. He looked up from his desk.

'Great picture, Mike. Well done.'

But no questions asked about the background, or the horror. He went back to his papers.

By then, the *Mirror* Mercy Mission was history anyway.

The Cap'n was always very generous with cigars. He stocked up on Havanas, only the best. Indeed, he kept on ordering them even though he gave up smoking three years before his death. The selection included Punch *Churchills* (seven inches long, ring gauge 47mm), Montecristo *Especial No 2* (six inches long, ring gauge 38mm) and, if we were lucky, the Trinidad *Especials*, which were a personal favourite of Fidel Castro.

Now I happen to like cigars, too, which was almost my undoing while I was still finding my feet as his personal photographer.

It was this taste for Havanas that could have got me fired. In fact, I actually thought I'd be shown the door on the spot, a fate which befell more than one *Mirror* man who overstepped the mark.

One summer's day in 1985 I returned to the office after a particularly good lunch in a Fleet Street hostelry.

'I'm in the mood for a nice fat Havana,' I actually said aloud as I pushed through the swing doors into the black marble foyer – speaking to myself, as one tends to in this condition.

With my security card I activated the private door that separated the *Mirror* offices from Maxwell House. It led me to a lift accessible only to those who enjoyed the Boss's confidence.

The Chairman kept his cigars in a humidor in his private dining-room. And I felt like one.

So, in this rash moment fuelled with wine, *bonhomie* and Dutch courage, I thought: *why not?*

I turned the key, took the lift to the Ninth Floor, and stepped out into the brooding silence of the inner sanctum – a thickly carpeted ante-chamber leading to Bob's private quarters.

In front of me, the dining-room, lounge and bedroom doors were all locked. But . . . there was another way in. A secret door from the kitchen that only the staff knew about, and which opened directly into the dining-room.

The dining-room meant cigars – from R.M.'s private stock.

That secret door looked like part of the cream-painted kitchen wall. In the dining-room, from the other side, it merged with the flocked burgundy-coloured wallpaper – so you had to know where to push to open it. I knew.

I pushed – and I was in. Unfortunately, so was Cap'n Bob.

I marched in – and stopped dead in my tracks.

There, to my horror, was silhouetted the huge frame of the publisher seated at the end of the dining-room table. A single lamp illuminated his face like a Hallowe'en pumpkin as he sifted through a pile of papers.

He stared up at me under the black eyebrows.

'What do you want, Mister?' he demanded.

Mister in that tone spelled trouble.

I'd been rumbled. There was nothing to say – except the truth. By now I had realised something else. The old adage: *Never bullshit a bullshitter!*

I raised my hands high in mock surrender. And said, loudly and firmly: 'I've just had a fabulous lunch, R.M. and I fancied a cigar. I couldn't buy one in the restaurant – and I know you've got hundreds of them –'

There was the briefest of pauses.

'Take your cigar,' said the big man, 'and fuck off!'

But as I reached for the humidor he allowed himself the faintest flicker of a smile.

Twenty-nine September 1985. Sunday. Brixton is in flames.

The infamous riots that scarred South London on Saturday night have taken their toll. Now the *Daily Mirror* decide they need aerial photographs of the devastation that followed this orgy of violence.

What better vehicle to commandeer than Cap'n Bob's personal helicopter?

'Use the chopper whenever you want, Mike,' the Chairman had told me in a rash moment. He tended to say things like that, and mean them at the time. Even if he would as often as not retract them later.

But for now, the invitation stood. So I took him at his word.

'We'll take the chopper,' I said.

'Shouldn't we get the Old Man's approval?' queried a faint heart from the Picture Desk, as I checked my camera bag beside him.

'Certainly not,' I said loudly, exuding all the authority of R.M.'s personal lensman. 'As long as he's not using it, no problem. Let's just do it. We can argue about it later.'

Later we would. Later still, I would discover that MCC (Maxwell Communications Corporation, our umbrella company) would invoice their own paper for use of the whirly-bird – at £150 an hour.

Someone was making money, but don't ask me who, how, or where.

Right now I just needed to get airborne, and in a hurry.

I checked with Maxwell's office. No answer.

Of course, it was Sunday. No one would be in unless the Boss summoned them. I had no idea where he was, but imagined he would be at his Oxfordshire country home, Headington Hill Hall. So I called up Dick Cowley, the pilot, on his mobile. He could be with me in half an hour.

A veteran reporter, Ron Ricketts, had been assigned to me. Thirty minutes later we were heading for the roof, and the now familiar astro-turf pad. The helicopter was there, its rotors turning, and Dick Cowley waiting at the controls.

'What's happening?' he asked. A map of the city was spread out on his lap.

I filled him in. 'We're heading for Brixton. I'll need to get down as low as possible.'

'Okay!' Dick knew what he could do, and what he couldn't do.

It may not be common knowledge, but the permitted minimum height of a helicopter joy-riding across the rooftops of London is 1,500 feet. Any lower than that, and you are in trouble – big trouble, with a hefty fine at the end of it.

Also, as far as possible, a chopper has to follow a meandering route above the Thames, presumably in case something falls off or the pilot has to ditch.

Dick, professional as always, obtained permission to head for South London. Charlie 2, the call sign for the *Mirror*'s airborne steed, was on its way.

From the air, Brixton looked like just another tangle of streets instead of the war zone it had become overnight. You couldn't see the broken glass littering the pavements, the shattered shop-fronts, or the scorch marks from the fires. At least, not at that height.

I had to get closer.

The door was clamped wide open. Excellent. For visual contact, I needed unimpeded vision. Clutching my heavy Canon camera with the 400mm zoom lens, I made my way unsteadily across the vibrating floor of Charlie 2, clipped a cross-over harness of canvas and Velcro across my chest to a pair of steel D-rings on the door, and gingerly sat myself down on the edge.

Then I stuck my legs out into empty space, letting them dangle over the side.

Above me, the rotors roared.

I lined up the camera between my legs and focused on the fire-bombed devastation of a night of madness.

Still not close enough.

I shouted at Dick: 'Dive, dive, dive!' It sounded like the Japanese pilots going down on Pearl Harbor. The streets of Brixton raced up at me, and I snapped away like a lunatic, getting anything and everything on to celluloid.

From up front, Dick turned an apprehensive face to me. We had three minutes before Heathrow's radar started making waves.

'One more time!' I shouted.

'All right – but make it quick!'

With which the helicopter banked sharply, to give me a brilliant bird's-eye view of the carnage below.

Click! Click! Click!

Uh!-uh!

But a little too brilliant, because out of the helicopter tumbled yours truly! Christ!

I found myself dangling from a great height, with nothing between me and the gutters of Brixton except 1,000 feet of space.

What had happened was simple. I was so intent on getting the pictures that I had forgotten about something called the law of gravity and literally slipped out of the helicopter.

Silly, really. But here I was, hanging helplessly in mid-air, and shouting inanely. But still clinging on to my 400mm lens. After all, they do cost £2,000 each.

'Help! Help!'

The streets of South London oscillated slowly far below.

'Help-p-p!'

After what seemed an eternity but was probably only seconds, Ron's willing hands grabbed me and hauled me back into the cabin. I lay back in the seat, gasping like a fresh-caught trout.

Dick was on the radio, speaking urgently into it as we raced back to Maxwell House. The reporter was scribbling excitedly in his notebook. Me, I was shaking like a leaf.

As the wheels settled, the steel door to the stairwell opened – and the slim figure of Joseph the Portuguese staff butler emerged in his black jacket and pinstripe trousers, gravely bearing a tray with a large goblet of brandy on it.

So that was the reason for the radio call! Good old Dick – he thought of everything.

Joseph handed the goblet up to me in the cabin, and I swallowed the contents in about two gulps.

Finally I felt able to take the roll of film down to the dark room for processing – then headed smartly back to the kitchen.

Joseph poured me another of the Chairman's best Hennessy XO. A stiff one. I was still shaking, and probably speaking over-loudly as I regaled him with my exploits as a latter-day Harold Lloyd.

Catching a glimpse of my reflection in the mirror I saw a pale ghost looking back at me.

At which point a familiar bulk loomed large in the doorway. Cap'n Bob in person. He hadn't been in the country, after all – but in the next room presumably catching up with some work.

He greeted me with the concern of a father to a favourite son. 'What the fuck's going on?'

Then, seeing my complexion, he softened. 'It's all right, Mike. Help yourself. I've heard what happened.'

News travels fast.

'I'll bet you shit your trousers!'

The briefest of pauses while he summoned a witty punch-line. Then: 'Were you wearing white underpants, Mister? Well, they can't be white any more!'

His bellows of laughter echoed down the corridor. As I've indicated, Cap'n Bob's humour could be quite basic at times.

At least my picture took up most of page one.

CHAPTER THREE

The Games Afoot!

The Commonwealth Games, Edinburgh, July 1986. Robert Maxwell was Chairman – 'and the saviour', as he insisted on telling everyone.

As the hours ticked away in that long hot summer towards the opening ceremony, the directors of the Commonwealth Games Scotland 1986 Ltd were in an understandable state of panic.

For six years, everyone had known that the Games were coming to Edinburgh. It was in every paper in the land at some time or other. Posters were prepared. Hotels waited for the great influx.

But right up to 1983 the entire staff of CGS Ltd consisted of just one typist.

Worse was to come. Television rights were undersold, even though there was great talk of 'media exposure to one billion people'. The BBC snapped up the rights for just £500,000.

There was a row over the mascot. An original bizarre idea of a grey seal emblem was changed to a Scottie dog, and the PR firm who suggested the seal was fired.

Then several African countries pulled a moody, protesting against the inclusion of South Africa, and started dropping off like flies. In all, ten would boycott the great event.

Then some bright spark said: 'All it takes is the inspired leadership of one individual to make this work!' And that was all it took to sound the clarion call which Cap'n Bob would answer.

Enter the White Knight.

Bob took over as chairman on 19 June. Telegrams went winging off to the disenchanted African states, to no visible avail.

But he managed to produce a Japanese philanthropist named Ryoichi Sasakawa, and persuaded the hon. gentleman from the Land of the Rising

Sun to chip in two million pounds.

Bob also produced Mirror Group Newspaper matchboxes that said: 'Forward with Britain'. Closer inspection revealed they were MADE IN JAPAN.

Stern telegrams to the Heads of African States reminded them: 'These are not Margaret Thatcher's Games, not even my Games. These Games belong to the Commonwealth.'

Nice try. The Saviour was pulling every iron out of the fire – and ramming them up numerous posteriors to save the day.

All right, it didn't work. But watching at close hand as Cap'n Bob unleashed his formidable energies and vast resources on this one pet project was an awesome spectacle.

'We'll do it, Mike,' he said, exuding confidence at his desk, poring over the plans, 'and I want you there to record it. Don't stray far away.'

Ostensibly, Cap'n Bob had taken on the Games for one reason only. 'Think of the humiliation to the country if Edinburgh had gone into receivership. I couldn't allow that. Remember, I am British by choice. Most people are British by accident.'

No one could guess then that at the end of the day the White Knight would ride off into the sunset leaving a £3.8 million debt behind – for someone else to pay.

Actually he would limp off. He had broken his left ankle climbing into the helicopter on his way to see the men's final at Wimbledon a few days earlier. Now he had to support his considerable weight on a stout black walking stick that ironically had been given to him by an African leader who stayed away. I was tempted to call him Bwana, but stuck with R.M. Well, it was safer.

But give the big man credit: he had tried, with a personal crusade of arm-twisting and cajoling to make it work. No one on this planet could have done more.

And in the end, God knows how, it did work.

We were booked in to the Sheraton Hotel on Festival Square, a stylish five-star emporium near the city centre with coloured fountains playing in the courtyard outside and 261 rooms inside at £100 a night, minimum whack.

Scottish ambience abounded. Strains of the odd piper filtered through the foyer, and I rather liked their motto: 'Step into a different world of stylish elegance and superior service in the grand Scottish tradition.'

The Chairman's idea of stylish elegance was somewhat out of step with that of the hotel. He had rented the Diplomatic Suite for himself at £580 a night, a figure which would rise to a grandiose £1,500 a night by the time we checked out, largely due to his lavish hospitality.

But the Games started well, considering the boycott from the African

With Prince Charles and Princess Diana at the Commonwealth Games.

states and the ridicule that rivals had tried to foster in their wake.

Sample? Some cartoonist in the *Listener* had jibed: 'Poor old Maxwell. Losing athletes faster than readers!'

But the publicity – which was all that mattered to the Saviour – made world headlines. Not just for what was going on in the field, but for the backstabbing and political to-ing and fro-ing that would run riot off the track.

For now, on this opening day, Cap'n Bob was in his element. The Queen was there. Prince Charles and Princess Di had looked in and signed the visitors' book before looking out again. Prince Andrew and Fergie would be along. Oh, and let's not forget the Prime Minister, Margaret Thatcher.

Under the summer sun, the great outdoor Meadowbank Stadium had been abuzz with excitement as the athletes paraded past the VIP podium.

Now it was early evening, and I found myself introducing the Chairman to Her Majesty.

How so?

As personal photographer to the Chairman of the Commonwealth Games, I had been given a VIP pass, and became the only lensman allowed behind the ropes into the royal enclosure.

This gave me access to the inner sanctum of power and privilege, which turned out to be a hospitality suite where the great and the good were on muster, hoping to catch the royal eye and shake the royal mitt.

A face that would become familiar to the public was eagerly bobbing at R.M.'s elbow like a tug nudging the *QE2* – Malcolm Rifkind, then Secretary of State for Scotland, was jostling to be noticed.

For once, I was on higher ground than the Cap'n because I had actually told the Queen a joke, and survived to tell the tale again – and again.

'You told the Queen a *joke*?'

'Yes, R.M., I did.'

'Let me hear it.'

Even the Boss was taken aback when I regaled him with the story two hours later, back in his suite. But that was how I had been able to effect the introduction he craved.

An explanation is necessary.

It had been a couple of years previously, when I was covering a two-month royal tour of Australia, New Zealand and the Far East.

One of the more pleasant (and least-known) traditions has it that every time the royal yacht *Britannia* heaves to in a new harbour, the travelling and local Press are invited aboard to take cocktails with the royal visitor.

This time the arena was Melbourne, down under in Oz. It was early evening, with pre-dinner cocktails on board *Britannia* – an event in itself. The great ship was bedecked with lights. The crew never speak – but communicate with hand signals. Spooky – but somehow terribly British.

The Queen's Press Secretary, Michael Shea, was on hand to introduce the exclusive group of guests from the Fourth Estate to Her Majesty. Eleven of us from the UK, coupled with back-up from the local Kangaroo Press. In all, no more than 20 of us.

The Queen was awaiting us in an ante-room for the formal introductions as we filed in. We were ushered through like so many lambs, and then moved on into the wardroom for cocktails and a further chance to chat with the royal personage. A bow here, a scrape there.

Protocol is everything. 'You must call her Your Majesty the first time. Then afterwards it's Ma'am,' is the stern instruction. 'And on no account do you approach the Queen – she will approach you if she wishes to talk to you.'

My turn. I bow low (she is quite petite) and shake the Queen's white-gloved hand. Then I pass on into the wardroom, where a uniformed steward stationed at the door proffers gin-and-tonic from a silver tray.

We stand in small groups awaiting the royal presence, making extremely small talk in suitably hushed tones, as if in a cathedral. You can cut the atmosphere with the proverbial knife.

The presence of royalty has an extraordinary effect on people, and I always wonder why. Whether it's a Royal Film Performance at the Odeon, Leicester Square, a Royal Gala at the Opera House in Covent Garden, or even one of those Royal Variety Shows at the Palladium, that dreadful silence is waiting to fall like a heavy shroud when the royal guest appears.

Personally, I always feel a twinge of sympathy. It must be like walking into a wall, with every syllable carrying its clearly audible sound to the assembled line-up like peas dropping into a metal bowl.

But there I stood with my polished shoes enmeshed in the thick carpet of the wardroom aboard the royal yacht *Britannia* pondering the possibility of telling the Queen a joke.

It would be a first – and possibly a last. But it had always been an ambition of mine, and as the humorist of the party I had had some success with my stories among the Press Corps. In short, I fancied my chances. 'I'll bet you won't,' said Chris Buckland, my *Mirror* colleague, when I confided my intentions to him.

'If the opportunity comes, I will!' I promised him.

And suddenly there she was in front of me, a small figure in a silk cocktail dress – but with enormous presence. A pair of flinty blue eyes fixed themselves on me.

Michael Shea murmured in her ear.

'Mr Maloney? Ah . . . And how are you enjoying Australia?' she inquired solicitously.

'Very much, thank you ma'am,' I replied, mindful of the other instruction to rhyme ma'am with *jam* – not with *calm*.

'And are you enjoying the food?' she pursued, totally out of the blue.

Aha! My chance had come, fortified by a couple of those *Britannia* measure g-and-ts, which is a tumbler with at least three units of gin, and not a lot of tonic.

'Well, ma'am,' I tell her. 'We had a somewhat unusual Chinese meal last night, with a waiter who didn't speak very good English.'

'Oh, really?' The royal features remain impassive.

'Yes,' I continue, realising that I have now passed the point of no return. At her shoulder I glimpse the Press Secretary's face darkening like an impending thunder-cloud as he senses what is coming.

'He asked me: "What you like?"' (Here I screw up my eyes, and put on my best Charlie Chan accent.)

Standing less than three feet from Her Majesty, I flap my elbows, emitting curious clucking sounds. 'I told him: "I want *cluck-cluck-cluck* soup!"'

'"Ah!" said the Chinese waiter, his face lightening with comprehension. "You want chicken soup?"'

'"No," I told him. "I want mushroom soup."'

'He looked baffled. "Ah? Then why you make sound like *cluck-cluck-cluck* chicken?" More windmilling of arms.

'"Because I can't make a sound like a mushroom,"' I replied.

There is a long, ominous pause, the kind of pause where you can hear the blood flowing in your veins. Michael Shea's face has turned to stone. Suddenly the *Britannia* has taken on the aura of a tomb.

Then, from nowhere, a high-pitched sound fills the wardroom. It comes from the Queen. She is laughing, her voice the wail of a tiny banshee, rocking back and forth on her heels like one of those weighted dolls you can never push over.

But it is enough to break the spell. In seconds the members of her entourage are joining in, rocking and laughing like a spiritual revival meeting.

My neck is safe. No date with the Tower. The atmosphere lightens on the spot.

How could I know that two years later this would be the key to my introducing the Monarch to the Boss? Even if, afterwards, Michael Shea took my elbow and said grimly: 'Don't you ever pull a trick like that again!'

Backstage at the Meadowbank Stadium, even Cap'n Bob was looking nervous – a condition as rare as a sighting of the great bustard. Inside the VIP Room, he paced up and down. Her Majesty was due any minute.

I stood by the door waiting to take the pictures that would end up framed in his office and in his various homes. As one of the accredited officers, I was decked out in a natty navy-blue blazer, grey flannels, Commonwealth Games tie, and embroidered red-and-white Commonwealth Games badge emblazoned on my breast pocket.

A stirring at the doorway – and in stepped the Queen, wearing an elegant burgundy suit and black hat with a matching burgundy band. She spotted me. Possibly because I was the first person in her path.

'Oh, hello!' A radiant smile. 'How are you?'

'Very well indeed, Your Majesty. And – ' I turned to Cap'n Bob – 'You know Robert Maxwell, of course.'

'Of course!' She extended a hand, and the Chairman bowed low over it.

'Permit me to present you with a token of this great event that I have orchestrated,' he said heavily, producing a limited edition coin-set laid out in a magnificent bound box.

Her Majesty accepted it with another beaming smile, the kind you don't see that often. Bob was beaming too – 'like a corgi with three tails', as someone remarked later, well out of his hearing.

The atmosphere was positively euphoric. The Queen was obviously enjoying the occasion, and the two of them chatted away like old friends. From the expression on Bob's face, he could already see himself breasting the tape to a knighthood.

Eventually Her Majesty made her excuses. A flunkey clutched the coin box under his arm as she was ushered out across the red carpet and into a rainy Edinburgh evening. The Chairman hastened to escort her, holding a large striped umbrella to protect the royal trilby from the elements.

Once she was in the car and he had bowed her away, he turned to me.

'Let's go!' he barked.

And we went . . . as far as the pavement outside the arena where his limousine should have been waiting. Except that it wasn't.

Back in the arena, the Games were still going on. Athletes were running, jumping and striving for gold. But out here the whole area was curiously bereft of transport – not a car in sight, not a taxi, nothing. The smile faded from Bob's face.

'Shall I call for a taxi, R.M.?' I ventured.

'No,' he said shortly. 'Follow me!'

And off he limped down a windswept passage to the busy main road.

Maxwell was never a man to hang around, not for a minute. And especially so when he was getting soaked to the skin. Without warning he jumped into the road and strode into the middle of the highway, raising an imperious hand to stop the first vehicle coming towards us.

A large black Rover slewed to a halt.

'I am Robert Maxwell, the Chairman of the Commonwealth Games,' the Cap'n announced in stentorian tones through the closed window to the startled driver. 'This is a matter of the utmost urgency. Take me immediately to the Sheraton Hotel.'

R.M. greets H.M.

R.M. escorts H.M.

The driver's pale face swam up at us through the rain. 'I know who you are, Mr Maxwell. But I am committed to Mr Ronald Jones (whose name I vaguely recalled as a Captain of Industry at the Games). I'm picking him up at the stadium.'

'No you're not.' The Chairman was already in the car. Without ceremony he had pulled open the door and before the driver had finished his sentence he was squeezed into the rear of the vehicle, beckoning me to follow.

'Don't worry,' the big man said portentously. 'I will give you a letter to your boss.'

To me, he said: 'Mike, take dictation!'

I fumbled for a pen and a piece of paper. The Cap'n proceeded to dictate a letter of absolution to the hapless sinner at the wheel, which I scribbled down as best I could.

Bob read the letter. 'Excellent,' he said. And signed it on the spot.

He leaned forward. 'Give this to your boss. He will understand,' was all he said, and sat back on the cushions, smiling in satisfaction.

In the lobby of the hotel, with the evening stretching ahead of us, the Chairman put a meaty arm around my shoulder, always a good sign that I must have done something right, and beamed at me.

'I must say that I'm very pleased with the way you operate, Mike,' he said gruffly. 'Join me for dinner tonight.'

It was a command rather than an invitation. Come to think of it, I never heard Bob say 'please' in his life.

'What do you like to eat?'

I've always been partial to the taste of the Orient, and this was to play a large part in my gastronomic future – or astronomic, when I think of the bills – with the Boss.

'I rather like Chinese food, R.M.'

'Hmm,' he said. Then: 'Yes, I like that too.'

I accompanied him to the Diplomatic Suite. Somehow it seemed odd to be looking for Chinese food in Scotland. But the Chairman strode over to the phone, and rang the manager.

'What's the name of your best Chinese restaurant in Edinburgh?' he demanded.

Pause. Then: 'Order me a takeaway meal for 12 people at eight o'clock sharp, here in my suite.' That would be in half an hour.

I heard a tremulous Scots voice down the line. 'Mr Maxwell, I'm afraid they don't do takeaways.'

The Boss's brows knitted. 'Tell them it's for me – and they *will*.' And he put the phone down.

Five minutes later the bell rang. The hotel manager again. 'Mr Maxwell, they will do it for you.'

Cap'n Bob nodded in satisfaction.

'But . . . we've got a problem collecting the food – '

'Problem – ?' The Boss didn't like that one bit.

'Yes, sir. We don't have any cars, and there are no taxis. They're all at the stadium.'

Maxwell's face darkened like a tropical storm. *'How do you come to work, Mister?'*

The voice was even more high-pitched. 'On my motor-bike, Mr Maxwell.'

'Then fetch the fucking food on your motor-bike!'

And slam! Down went the phone.

It was there at eight on the dot. The manager had indeed got on his bike – and piled cartons into twin panniers on either side of his saddle. By the time I presented myself at the Diplomatic Suite on the seventh floor, showered and changed, the feast was laid out waiting. A long table had in fact been set for 14, with six chairs on either side and one at each end. Crisp white cloth. Places laid out neatly with gleaming plates, wine glasses and chopsticks.

The food was in dishes with silver lids on to keep them warm, and there was enough of it to feed 20.

Beyond the table, the view from the picture windows stretched across the city to the Castle, where I could see a flag fluttering above the tower, its great stone ramparts tinted rose pink in the setting sun. A magnificent sight.

The Boss was already there. He had not waited for his guests, and somehow I doubted if he had spent a lot of time admiring the view. Instead he was standing by the table stuffing a large egg roll into his mouth.

'Co' . . . in . . . Ha' . . . a . . . glass . . . o' . . . DP,' he said indistinctly.

I counted eight bottles of Dom Perignon nestling in ice buckets around the table. Two waitresses who had laid it all out were hanging nervously around by the sideboard. Bob dismissed them with a wave of his hand.

Then he gestured at the chairs. Through a mouthful of egg roll he said: "oo si' ther'. I'll si' her'!' And plumped himself heavily down at the far end.

I took my seat at the opposite end, and poured myself a glass of bubbly, wondering when the other guests would make an appearance.

'Who else is coming, R.M.?' I ventured aross the intervening space.

'What do you mean?' He seemed surprised at the thought. 'There's no one else. Dive in, help yourself!'

Who was I to disobey the high command?

As I picked up the chopsticks and delicately fastened on a shrimp, my host's huge hands suddenly shot out from his sleeves, hovered over the nearest

With Prince Edward at the Games. Jean Baddeley and Debbie Dines are on the right.

dishes, then dived. I was reminded of those mechanical grabbers you see on building sites.

I watched as my Chairman scooped up handfuls of grilled prawns and chow mein, and literally stuffed them into his mouth as if he'd been on a starvation diet for a month. It was a stomach-churning sight – but one I would grow used to seeing over the years to come.

57

Cap'n Bob seldom, if ever, bothered with the niceties of culinary etiquette. Talking with his mouth full, spraying his guests with the costly delicacies he was providing for them, was something his inner circle had learned to endure.

'Funny thing, Publisher,' I ventured.

'Wha', Mike . . . ?'

'Funny thing that we should be eating Chinese now, and we've just met the Queen.'

The Chairman paused briefly and looked down the table at me, his cheeks bulging like small cushions. 'Huh?'

'Well, ' I said. 'That joke I told her . . . '

'Oh, yes, that.' He returned to his plate.

As every stand-up comic knows, it's great to be appreciated.

For the next 20 minutes we sat there in virtual silence, broken only by the chomping sounds from the far end of the table.

Finally the Boss had had his fill. He had guzzled down enough Chinese food for six, along with copious quantities of champagne, and his boredom threshold was always on the low side, anyway.

My efforts at conversation had petered out with a grunt or a mutter from the far end. Eventually I gave up.

At last he stood up, and headed for the bedroom. I stood up too.

At the door, mine host turned and waved a hand.

'Finish this off. Help yourself to the champagne. And . . . ' The gesture took in a large humidor on the sideboard . . . 'I know you like my cigars.'

The door shut behind him.

I finished the meal alone, aided by several glasses of DP. I didn't even switch on the television for company. Then I took the biggest Havana I could find, and swayed off to bed.

I just hoped there were enough cats in Edinburgh to do justice to the leftovers.

Halfway through the Games, the Chairman decided to hold a party for chosen delegates and officials in the Diplomatic Suite at the Sheraton. It was early evening and I was in the suite with Bob awaiting the first arrivals, when he reached for the phone. He put a call through to his trusted chauffeur and right-hand man, Les Williams. Known to us all simply as Les, he was a big, affable man who always stayed in tip-top condition so that he could act both as driver and minder to the Boss.

'Get me some chicken legs,' Maxwell commanded. 'Enough for 30 people.'

The delegates started to flock in. The Dom Perignon, magnums of it, started to flow. The men in their smart blue blazers, the ladies in cocktail dresses, warmed to the occasion.

You could almost sense the taste buds salivating as they waited for the food from their benefactor, whose largesse in times of triumph had become legendary.

Beluga caviar? Foie gras? What would it be tonight?

The door opened. In marched Les, followed by a couple of waiters. My eyes widened, as did those of everyone in the room.

Clutched in their arms, like trophies from a summer sale, were cardboard tubs filled with chicken legs – 'Kentucky Fried Bargain Buckets', each tub containing 20 portions.

As a stark silence fell, I counted 14 buckets.

'Oh, there they are!' our host exclaimed jubilantly. 'Over here, Les!'

And he seized the first Bargain Bucket, dipped in a big paw, and proceeded to dole out the contents to his guests by hand. He didn't even use a paper serviette.

'Dive in, everyboby!'

To my horror, I noticed the Cap'n take a large bite out of a crisply fried leg himself before handing it on to a startled guest. 'Here, try this!'

The first recipient was a lady who was too stunned to refuse. As were the others who were recipients of Bob's generosity – along with the imprint of the great man's teeth. There was one saving grace, I suppose. At least the teeth were his own.

That summer was eventful in more ways than one. But then, working alongside Cap'n Bob, I suppose all my summers were – and the rest of the year besides.

Take the Derby that year. They had a streaker for the first time in the history of that great race. As my Chairman, hosting a luncheon party for 22 guests in the MCC private box would put it later: 'At least that suffragette who threw herself under the hooves at Tattenham Corner had the decency to keep her clothes on!'

I was fortunate enough to be invited, resplendent along with the other male guests in morning suit, to find a typically lavish Maxwell occasion – champagne reception, cold salmon and chablis *Premier Cru*. The other guests seemed to be mostly from the City, which figured.

I had my camera, of course, ready to spring into action if the Chairman wanted a picture with a particular big-wig.

I excused myself for the two main races, the 3.45 p.m. Derby itself and the one that preceded it, the Coronation Stakes, as the others went out on to the balcony above the stand to watch.

'You point it this way, Bob!' (picture by Senator Howard Baker, White House)

The first race finished. I was positioned by the winning post, took a few snaps, and was watching the tails of the last horses disappearing into the middle-distance when suddenly a mighty roar went up from the stands. I looked up the course – to see a man rush out on to the grass, stark naked! Police and stewards were in hot pursuit, and more of the boys in blue came from all around me to join in the chase.

I went with them. In full morning dress, clutching my camera, heading for the first furlong mark where the streaker was still running, eluding the grasp of outstretched hands with whoops of triumph. I arrived just as they did catch him, to carry him off with a blue helmet placed over the appropriate vital area. Another page one!

I heard a shout above the hubbub and looked up to find I was right opposite the Chairman's box – and there was Cap'n Bob on the balcony with his pals, laughing and gesturing at me like one of the tic-tac men down below.

Dimly I caught his voice 'That's my boy!'

I trust he was referring to me and not the streaker.

CHAPTER FOUR

God Bless America!

A warm summer's evening by the Great Lakes in June 1990. We are in Minnesota, U.S.A., driving through the city of St Paul, the State capital, in a stretch limousine that was so big you needed binoculars to see the chauffeur up front.

At least, that was my joke to the Chairman as we sat in cushioned luxury in the rear, to be received with the usual grunt of disinterest.

For once, the usual entourage is missing. Bob and myself, just the two of us, have been invited to the home of the fourth richest man in America – one Whitney McMillan, a farmer, and no relation to the giant publishing house of Macmillan which Bob had taken over in November 1988 after a bruising battle and a resulting hole in his wallet amounting to £1.4 billion.

For Farmer Whitney, these matters were of passing interest. He wanted to meet Bob, and the feeling was mutual. Two rich men. Two very rich men.

We – that is, the Cap'n and myself – were also due to have lunch next day with a certain Mikhail Gorbachev, President of Russia. I was masquerading, not for the first (or last) time, as Mrs Robert Maxwell. By now, I was used to this charade. Mrs M. had other things to occupy her life, and Bob wanted me along with my camera.

This time the gilt-edged invitation requested the company of Mr and Mrs Robert Maxwell for dinner. Bob was the guest of honour.

The problem for both of us was that we had just disembarked from Gulfstream 2 after flying the Atlantic, via Ganda in Newfoundland for the usual refuelling. In short, and without wishing to be crude, we were both knackered. Even Bob's incredible stamina was feeling the strain.

We had arrived that afternoon at 3 p.m., and somehow stayed awake until 7 p.m. for our dinner date. Which meant that as far as our stomachs were concerned, the soup would be served at midnight U.K. time. Looking out at the passing landscape, as the streets of the inner city gave way to leafy suburbs, I wondered whether St Paul would turn out to be one of the less exciting places where Cap'n Bob and I would set foot in our travels.

The city straddled the Mississippi, which was the first surprise – I had always associated that river with the Deep South, instead of the northernmost state of the United States outside Alaska. But there it was: Minnesota, lying next to Dakota and the Black Hills that Doris Day's silver tones once extolled in song.

Two-thirds prairie, producing cattle, meat and grain, with nickel and copper in the mountains by Lake Superior taking over from the old iron ore mines, and 11,000 small lakes for the tourists and the anglers.

We had bigger fish to fry. Our chauffeur-driven limousine scrunched up the drive outside a palatial mansion on the edge of town and disgorged us at the front door. As we climbed the steps, Bob suddenly said: 'No need to bother with pictures tonight, Mike.'

Oh? I thought how I'd much rather be tucked up in bed. But once again, I was there just for his company.

Inside was a maze of interlocking reception rooms, beneath glittering chandeliers, guests in dark suits and cocktail dresses (plus a load of jewellery) jostling for champagne cocktails, canapes and recognition. Someone murmurs that this is one of the season's top events, Minnesota high society on show.

Our host is grey-haired, elderly and affable. He looks more like a banker than a farmer. Whitney McMillan pumps my hand.

'Delighted to meet you, Mike.' No ceremony here.

I had been expecting an intimate soirée for a dozen people, maximum. Instead, all the downstairs rooms are packed with guests, all of them there to set eyes on the flavour-of-the-month publishing tycoon.

Bob starts to do the rounds, surging through the crowd like a Sherman tank. It's called networking – he never knew whose hand he might be shaking, but maybe that hand would be signing a deal by the time it had finished counting its fingers.

As for me, I'm fascinated by the fact that the man in front of me is one of the nation's largest farmers. He certainly doesn't look like America's answer to Dan Archer.

'They tell me you're the country's biggest farmer, sir,' I venture. 'May I ask how many people you employ?'

He pauses for a moment. Then replies: 'I guess about 420.'

'Oh, I was expecting a few more than that,' I say without thinking.

'Around here, son, 420,000 is a *lot* of employees,' and he gives me a chilly lop-sided grin to go with it.

Dinner at last. In London, it must be 2 a.m. In St Paul, my eyelids are starting to close. We are ushered in to an elegant dining-room, where a long table has been laid for a select 20.

In my guise of Mrs Maxwell, I find myself somewhat embarrassingly seated next to mine host at the centre of the table, with another male guest on my right. So much for the carefully orchestrated seating plan of man-woman-man!

In truth, it didn't worry me too much. By now I had grown used to being an 'item' with Cap'n Bob. It had happened before, and it would happen again.

My camera had remained tucked away in my overcoat outside. But looking around, marvelling at the style and opulence, I had a fleeting wish that I could have photographed the flower arrangements, the antique chairs, the oil paintings on the walls and the elegant ambience of the occasion in that magnificent room. Someone had gone to a lot of trouble for the honoured guest.

A waiter filled my glass with a delicious dry white Burgundy. The aroma of roast pheasant wafted through from the kitchens. My taste buds twitched.

Bob sat opposite me, flanked by two elderly ladies. I could see his large head beginning to nod. He was half asleep. Looking at him, I was less worried by my initial goof with Dan Archer than with the sudden prospect of the Chairman burying his face in the Caesar's salad.

I have already said that Cap'n Bob had enormous resilience, more than any man I ever met. He followed Churchill's principle: always take a cat-nap when you can.

But there was a limit even to his stamina.

Suddenly, he came alert.

Without warning he picked up a big silver soup spoon, and banged it noisily on the tablecloth.

A deathly hush descended. On my left, Whitney stopped what he was saying in mid-sentence.

The Chairman lumbered to his feet. His booming tones went through the niceties of thanking his host for 'such a wonderful evening', and went on to elaborate on why he was in 'this wonderful part of the world', adding that he had a 'very important meeting' next day: with President Mikhail Gorbachev.

'You'll forgive me, ladies and gentlemen, if I have to leave now. I also have some urgent phone calls which I have to make to London.'

Our host and I rose too, and followed his huge bulk out of the room in a silence of both astonishment and disbelief.

'Sorry you couldn't stay, Bob,' said Whitney.

'So am I, Whit,' said the Chairman, scrambling into the back seat of the stretch limo.

I watched Farmer McMillan's perplexed face disappear into the darkness, thinking to myself that all I'd had to show for the evening was half a glass of white wine and a lettuce leaf.

'I have to say, R.M.,' I said. 'I feel absolutely zonked out.'

Cap'n Bob was ahead of me. He had upset our host, quite without intention or even realising it. He had left the guests open-mouthed, and he had walked out before the main course. In short, it had been another average night. A loud snore filled the limo. Now he was fast asleep.

Next morning, bright and early, we were up and about at dawn. The hotel breakfast room opened at 7 a.m. Eggs over-easy, hash-brown potatoes, crisp bacon, as much coffee as you could drink. They call it 'bottomless coffee' – and so are you after drinking it. I always did like a big breakfast on a big day. And this was going to be a *mega* day.

I knew the Boss would be awake. Frequently he could manage on two or three hours a night, and his body clock would be registering 11 a.m. London time anyway.

To quote Bob: 'All great leaders in history, Mike, have existed on three hours sleep a night. Napoleon, Churchill, Margaret Thatcher. And me.'

'Yes, R.M.,' I would respond dutifully, thinking of the eight hours I personally prefer.

I knocked on the door of the penthouse suite.

'Come!'

Inside, the Boss was in his shirt-sleeves.

'Ah, Mike. You're just in time for morning exercise!'

Exercise! This was a first. What on earth had he got in for me this time?

He pointed to the lift. 'Follow me!'

We proceeded to the hotel car park. Then we walked round a few cars. It must have taken us all of three minutes.

'There,' beamed the Boss in satisfaction. 'Don't you feel better for that? Now – let's go back to the suite.'

Upstairs, we discussed the pending Big Event.

Luncheon with Gorbachev, his wife Raisa, and with the State Governor Rudy Perpich and his wife Lola at the Governor's Residence at 1006 Summit Avenue. Plus a vast number of State dignitaries attending what, for them, would be the biggest event of the year. For some of them, probably, the event of their lives.

Gorby was on a State visit, basically a whistle-stop tour to shake hands, smile, and show that the Cold War was over and that the Russian Bear was a friendly animal after all.

Problem. Because of the near-paranoid security strictures, for once I wasn't on the guest list. Not even as Mrs Maxwell.

The world's Press would be out in force, and they had built a special stand to accommodate them outside the Governor's Residence across the road from the main entrance.

Even the Press Corps travelling with Gorby would be kept at least 50 yards away – and on the outside, looking in.

Cap'n Bob needed me on the inside, looking out.

'I want you there, Mike. I'm adamant. This is very important to me.

'But I haven't got a ticket, R.M. I've not even been invited.'

'We'll see about that!'

In fact there had only been two official invitations to the Maxwell Group for Minnesota's social event of the year: the Chairman himself, and the President of the American arm of Maxwell Communications Corporation, Bob Smith.

So many people had been fighting for a place that they had been forced to extend the banqueting room behind the main house into a huge marquee in the grounds.

I was aware that all the names would be on a security list, and that we would be certain to be rigorously checked.

'Er, Bob . . . '

'You'll come with me, Mister,' said the Chairman heavily.

Which is how, at 12.30 p.m., I found the Governor's personal stretch limousine waiting for us outside, complete with the Stars and Stripes fluttering on the bonnet. I strode down the hotel steps behind Bob, exuding confidence, part of the A-Team.

'Come!' ordered the Cap'n, and ducked inside, followed by the other Bob. Then followed by me.

'Mike, you sit in the middle.'

Plain Bob Smith was as rotund as his boss, but there was still plenty of room in the interior of that car. I sat in the middle between them, feeling like the filling in a sandwich.

The car headed for Summit Avenue.

A map on the invitations showed the route we had to take – one-way round the back streets of St Paul, taking the scenic path. To me it looked like just another mid-American town. We got an aerial view of it when Bob reached over and switched on the TV set that was positioned above the drinks cabinet, between the jump seats behind the driver.

'I see they're expecting us!'

They were, too. Helicopter shots showed Gorby meeting crowds of onlookers on his way to the luncheon. He would order his own car to stop, and emerge for a brief walkabout to press the flesh before hopping back inside.

I couldn't help noticing the number of suits milling around him in a protective scrum. FBI and Secret Service, standing out in any crowd with their short-back-and-sides haircuts and walkie-talkies. They couldn't afford to lose Minnesota's prize guest.

The first road block loomed up. Three police cars with golden stars on their sides, plus two motor-bike riders. And a lot of guns in evidence.

But, surprisingly, no problem.

Cap'n Bob put a large thumb on a button beside him, the electronic window slid down – and I could see our reflections in the menacing sun-glasses of the cop staring in at us.

Bob had his invitation in his hand. All he said was: *'Robert Maxwell!'* But he said it loudly.

It was enough. The cop stepped back without a word, and waved us on.
We're through!

Wrong.

One mile farther on, the same thing. Only this time the road block was even less hospitable.

'Names, gentlemen?' The helmeted head in the window spoke.

Again, the Chairman did the honours.

'Robert Maxwell.' He waved the invitation, gestured in our direction. 'Robert Smith. And Michael Maloney – whom the Governor is looking forward to seeing again!'

The cop searched our faces, then glanced at the invitations. The Boss was waving his card with all the vigour of a matador trying to distract a bull, and plain Bob Smith held his invite up on the far side like a talisman.

'Thank you, gentlemen.'

This time we were through. The limo glided past the serried ranks of the world's Press perched on their grandstand, and slid out of their sight up a short drive.

A footman opened the car doors. Cap'n Bob put a large foot on to the forecourt of the Governor's Residence. We were in. So were my cameras, nestling in their brown leather bag. No one had queried that, either.

The Chairman turned a beaming face to me. 'I told you so,' he said with satisfaction. Another quirk I'd noticed was his child-like delight in getting one over on authority.

Cap'n Bob had got me through the combined forces of the FBI, the Secret Service, the State troopers and the militia surrounding the second most powerful man in the world – and he was like a schoolboy.

Inside, Governor Rudy Perpich pumped Bob's hand in greeting. The

Chairman introduced his American aide, then me.

'Governor, this is Bob Smith. And you know the World's Greatest Photographer . . .'

He didn't use my name, and I knew why. He had forgotten it again. Cap'n Bob was atrocious on small details – like other people's names. By now I had learned not to take it personally.

Once, at a Labour Party conference, he introduced Mike Molloy, then Editor of the *Daily Mirror*, as 'Mick McGahey', much to the ribald amusement of his colleagues for weeks to come.

For now, I graciously accepted that the World's Greatest Photographer would have to do.

Rudy shook my hand. 'Of course I do. How are ya, Mike?' I had done some portraits of him months back, on his birthday, and he remembered my name, even if my boss didn't. He also remembered the ten-by-eight colour pictures I'd sent him as a memento of the occasion.

Politicians train themselves to remember, or at least to persuade their constituents that they do.

'I'm fine, sir, thank you.' The uninvited guest looked around, and felt he should say something appropriate to the occasion. 'I'm pleased to see the security's so tight around here.'

The Governor smiled in appreciation.

'It has to be,' he said. 'We can't take any chances.'

'Quite right,' chimed in Cap'n Bob, overhearing. He looked like the cat that had swallowed the cream.

Pre-lunch drinks. Some of the finest Chablis that had ever passed my palate arrived in leaded crystal glasses on trays borne by a horde of waiters.

'The President will be here in half an hour, Bob,' said the Governor. 'Why don't you go ahead and meet the folks.'

The folks were Minnesota's finest in the social strata, and they had come from all points of the compass. The State of Minnesota had been chosen to symbolise mid-America, and no one who mattered wanted to be left out.

I found myself rubbing shoulders with Congressmen, Senators, the cream of American high society and enough millionaires to buy out Fort Knox. I couldn't help noticing the Secret Service Suits with their cropped haircuts and hearing aids, quietly combing the rooms with hi-tech equipment in a sweep presumably for bugs and explosives.

Half an hour passed. Then another half hour.

Finally the signal came through. *'The President is five minutes away!'*

The informal cocktail party disintegrated in seconds.

'This way, please!' A brisk bespectacled female executive from Government

Office armed with a clipboard beckoned a chosen few out into the hall for the official presentation when Gorbachev would walk in through the big double doors.

There were only a dozen of them, including Cap'n Bob, and she ushered them into line like a schoolmistress. 'Please stand here . . . and here . . ' She read out the names.

Mine wasn't among them.

Well, not yet.

Maxwell was fourth in line, with Bob Smith next to him. Without being challenged, I took up a position facing him across the imposing pillared hallway.

One of those dreadful pin-drop silences fell that seem to go on for ever, heralding the arrival of somebody famous. Broken this time by the booming voice of Cap'n Bob, reverberating like thunder over a mountain range. *'Mr Snapper, are you ready?'*

'Absolutely, Chairman!'

'Gorby greeted him like an old friend.'

'Pleased to meet you, Mr President.'

The long, dragging silence deepened into the stillness of the graveyard. I felt it was time to lighten up.

So I stepped forward. 'Ladies and gentlemen,' I piped up, 'please remember to smile when you meet the President, as I will be photographing each one of you and the pictures will be appearing all over the world.'

The Boss liked that. A big smile came to his face, and he nodded approvingly. *Well done, Mike*, that smile said.

The big double doors opened. Six Suits strode in, and formed a human funnel, followed close behind by the familiar figures of Mikhail Gorbachev and his lovely wife Raisa.

The Russian President strode straight up to Rudy, and proffered his hand. With his interpreter close by, he proceeded to walk the line like a general inspecting his troops.

Fourth along was Cap'n Bob. Gorby greeted him like an old friend. Then moved on to the end – to find me facing him with a broad smile on my face and my hand extended.

'Mr President! So nice to meet you!'

I had nipped round the back of the line-up to take my place at the end. Well, the best form of defence is attack, I reasoned, and if I was the uninvited guest – best to disguise it upfront.

President Gorbachev, thank God, smiled back. He shook my hand energetically and eyed my camera. Through his interpreter he inquired solicitously: 'How are the photographs tonight?'

'Going fine, sir, thank you.'

Nice of him to ask. I was impressed. Bob Smith was impressed. Above all, Cap'n Bob was impressed.

The other guests had all been taking their places at tables laid for 12 in the ornate dining-room. The Governor and the guests of honour led the chosen few – which now included me – into the room, heading for the top table. Everyone stood and applauded. We all bowed in return.

Only one thing – there was no seat for me at that top table. But the lady with the clipboard saved the day. 'There's a place for you on Table 14,' she eyed me archly, 'whoever you are.'

The banquet was magnificent. Paté de foie gras vied for top billing with lobster thermidor, and strawberry Romanoff took the ring with Baked Alaska.

I chose my moment when everyone looked totally relaxed, then quietly approached the top table. Maxwell was sitting on Gorby's left, with Lola Perpich on the Russian President's other side and Raisa opposite, next to Rudy.

Suddenly Mikhail grabbed Bob's hand in a typically flamboyant Russian gesture of friendship. Later it transpired they were sealing an invitation for my

'Pleased to meet you, Mike!'

Chairman to be the guest of the USSR on a trip to Moscow in the near future.

Right now I was hovering discreetly behind Raisa's back, waiting for the right moment.

That's when I saw Gorby grab Bob's hand – not the other way round, as I might have expected – and snapped off a picture. In fact, several pictures.

They both looked up. Bob rumbled: 'Ah, Michael, there you are.' The smiles, at least, were mutual. Gorby extended a hand.

It had been close. Seconds later, everyone rose and made their way to the marquee outside to listen to the Russian President address them from the podium.

I was there before them. Positioned by the entrance, I saw Mikhail leading the way with Cap'n Bob trotting after in hot pursuit.

But suddenly the President spotted me, paused – and turned to shake my hand again.

'Michael!' Then, through his interpreter: 'I hope you will come to Moscow with your Chairman! You must take more pictures of my wife. An official portrait – at our home.' He paused, and a gleam came into his eye. 'You are the World's Greatest Photographer, I believe. Or so your Chairman assures me.'

With that accolade, how could Mr Snapper refuse?

The party was over. It was time to call it a day. Lunch long finished. Cutlery, crockery and tables cleared away. Speeches over. But Gorbachev was due to do yet another walkabout, downtown.

A fleet of official black bullet-proof limousines slid up outside the Governor's residence. Mikhail and Raisa stepped into the first vehicle, followed in the second car by Governor Rudy – and Cap'n Bob.

Mr Snapper jumped in too.

I took my place on one of the jump seats facing my Chairman and the Governor. It was a bullet-proof limo – but that didn't stop Bob from winding down the window to bestow a regal wave on the crowds clustered on the pavements.

We must have been travelling at a little over walking pace. I became aware of the sound of pounding footsteps – and into sight came a rugger scrum of eight men in flapping raincoats, keeping pace with our limousine. The Secret Service, answering the call.

I caught a glimpse of pistols nestling in holsters – and, rather more alarming, the outlines of Uzi machine-guns under the raincoats.

'Look at that, R.M.!'

'Ah, I see you've turned out the Praetorian Guard, Governor!'

Rudy nodded in mute affirmation.

That night, I made my big mistake. In the Presidential Suite at his hotel, four of us – the Cap'n, plain Bob Smith, myself and a personal assistant from the New York office – celebrated with Dom Perignon and Beluga caviar for the troops.

'That was brilliant, Bob,' I said, on the third glass of DP. I was referring to the occasion, and the lavish hospitality.

'Absolutely magnificent,' he echoed. 'Do you realise the deal I've just done with the President of Russia?'

'No,' I said, my curiosity roused. 'Can you tell me about it?'

Normally, I would never have asked.

'Yes I can.' Pause. 'But I'm not going to!' And that wicked grin appeared on his face that I had grown to know so well, taking the sting out of the words.

The mistake was to brag about the picture I had captured of Gorby grabbing his hand, a one-off if ever I saw one. Foolishly, I told him so.

Until then, he hadn't realised it had happened.

A silence fell while the Chairman digested the implications. I could see his mind working. That one picture would be worth a fortune for the Maxwell empire, to be used in the newspapers, the magazines, the books . . .

As for me, I might even get a Christmas bonus out of it.

'I want to see that picture,' he boomed. 'Now!'

At that hour, nothing was open.

'Get me the Yellow Pages,' he demanded. 'Find a laboratory that's open 24 hours. I want that picture! Find me somebody to process that film.'

And for the next 60 minutes, into the small hours, we searched and searched. In vain.

In the end we had to wait till next morning when we flew to New York. To find a helicopter waiting at White Plains to fly our precious cargo – the film, not us – to the centre of Manhattan. There a despatch rider was waiting to rush the film to the offices of Associated Press for processing. The prints came through an hour later. Maxwell was ecstatic.

'Well done, Mike. Now get them on the wire.'

They went post-haste to London for the Mirror Group Newspapers to mull over and print on page one.

They never saw the light of day.

'What's the matter, Mister?' Maxwell's antennae were on full alert. He could sense something was wrong.

'Well, R.M.' I hesitated.

'Go on!' He faced me across his suite at the Waldorf, fixing me with that unwavering stare.

'It's just a pity about the wine glasses obstructing the main point of the picture, R.M.'

'What do you mean, Mister?' He didn't like the sound of this one little bit. I wasn't too happy, either.

'Well . . . ' I tried to explain. 'Your hand in his. That's the picture we want – and we haven't quite got it.'

'That can be arranged.'

And it was.

Back in London, a photo-electronic laboratory came up trumps. With the miracle of modern cosmetic surgery, in those days practically unheard of, they erased the wine glasses – and 'painted in' the knives and forks.

The result, for the world to see: Gorby grabbing Bob's hand in a seal of everlasting comradeship.

That doctored single print would cost the firm £1,500. In the Boss's eyes, it was worth every extravagant penny. Back in Washington, more meetings, more socialising. Lunch with Senator Howard Baker, who is fascinated by photography, and has an impressive collection of Hasselblads, Nikons, Leicas, Cannons, so the pair of us got on famously.

Our arrival coincided with a big black-tie charity night being organised by Teddy Kennedy at one of the swish hotels. I recall that it was for AIDS, one of his pet (and politically correct) causes. And by big, I mean m-e-g-a. Teddy had been busy inviting all the top celebrities in Washington to buy tables, and other members of the Kennedy clan had rallied round to help make it a night to remember.

Bob heard of this. And, being Bob, made the magnanimous gesture, 'I will buy a table!'

Tables were for ten, there were only going to be ten of them, and they were 10,000 dollars a time. A whole lot of tens. Working out at 1,000 bucks a seat, and 100,000 dollars to the charity. It was a sell-out. The fact that there were only three of us – Bob, myself, and his bubbly assistant Andrea Martin, who had joined us – didn't faze the Cap'n one jot.

On the Saturday night we donned our best bib and tucker, climbed into the obligatory stretch limo, and headed off to the five-star Jefferson Hotel, one of Washington's finest. Cher was to be the cabaret, backed by a live orchestra. Other celebrities we were due to meet would include Muhammad Ali, Dr Ruth Westheimer the celebrity sex therapist, actress Ali McGraw and the *crème de la crème* of Washington high society. A varied bunch, you will agree.

Bob loomed large, in every sense. At the cocktail reception preceding the dinner, people came up from nowhere to shake his hand. The Cap'n was in his element, and on top form.

I introduced him to Muhammad Ali. 'This is the former heavyweight champion of the world, Mr Maxwell,' I knew when to be formal.

'Yes, I remember him. How do you do, Mr Clay.' Two famous heavyweights shook big paws in greeting.

'Actually, I prefer to be called Muhammad,' said Ali, somewhat stiffly.

To which my Chairman raised his fists, and squared up to the former champ. 'What are you going to do – hit me?' he boomed.

Oh, Christ! Cap'n Bob was in playful mood. Which almost inevitably heralded trouble. But Ali resisted the temptation.

'I always think of you as Cassius,' Bob went on, rubbing salt further into the wound. 'Why on earth did you change your name?'

Now you see it . . .

76

'Because I'm a Muslim.'

'Oh, are you?'

Somehow that was the end of *that* conversation.

I had a small Leica in my pocket, and would have given anything for that shot of the two of them together. But it was an occasion when photographers had been barred, so the camera had to stay where it was. For the moment.

We filed into the elegant chandelier-hung dining-room, and found our places. Wouldn't you know it? Our table had to be smack in the middle, an embarrassing island of space in a sea of black ties and cocktail dresses.

. . . now you don't!

Perhaps I was being over-sensitive, but from where I was sitting it looked as if we had been stood up by seven guests.

The Cap'n didn't notice. He polished off the first course – and then, bad sign, he started looking restless. I knew what was going to happen about ten seconds before it did.

'Let's go, Mike! Andrea . . . I'm off back to the hotel.'

I looked up from my prawn salad, aghast. 'R.M., please! I really would like to stay and see the cabaret.'

I could see he wasn't pleased, and pulled out my ace from the pack. 'I'm the only photographer here, and I can get some great pictures of Cher for the paper.'

That did it. 'Please yourself, Mister. Andrea and I will go back.'

That left me alone, feeling like a spare part at an otherwise empty table, surrounded by nine empty chairs and surveying a large expanse of white cloth and cutlery for the best part of the next two hours, with no one to talk to. Say hello to the Lonely Man!

But the food, at least, was out of this world. The main course was quail, and the wines were the finest that the Napa Valley in California could produce. A crumb of comfort, I thought, was that my 10,000 dollar meal was worth every cent.

It took a sex therapist to come to my rescue.

'Hey, Mike. You're looking kind of isolated out there!' Ruth, bless her, was at my elbow. In her early '60s, she had the energy of a woman half her age, a small dynamo with her German accent still intact after 35 years in the United States. She was dressed all in pink, and looked as if she had discovered the elixir of permanent youth. Perhaps she had.

'Come on over and join us at our table!'

I was only too glad to do so, and not just because I was fascinated to hear about books with titles like *Dr Ruth's Guide to Erotic and Sensuous Pleasures* and *The Art of Arousal*, or her radio show called *Sensually Speaking*.

Sensually speaking, I had only a few minutes to chat with the diminutive lady doctor before a drum roll heralded Cher's stupendous cabaret. The raven-haired stunner was dressed as daringly as ever, tonight in a skimpy black mini-number that left little or nothing to the imagination. That girl is shameless – but what a voice!

Halfway through, I slipped unobtrusively away to the side of the stage, and quietly snapped off 36 shots which would later appear in many of the Mirror Group's papers and magazines. For 10,000 dollars, it wasn't such a bad evening after all.

CHAPTER FIVE

Back in Uniform

Thursday, 31 August 1989, and an invitation in the form of a personal phone call to Maxwell's desk from General Wojciech Jaruzelski, the leader of the Polish Communist Party.

Would Bob care to attend the great national parade in Warsaw that they were planning to mark the fiftieth anniversary of the day the Germans marched into Poland?

Would he!

By now Jaruzelski had become quite a chum of the Chief. Indeed, I had already photographed them together a number of times.

Maxwell had endeared himself to the Polish hierarchy on an earlier trip to that economically beleaguered country, ostensibly to arrange for a Pergamon Press biography of General Jaruzelski himself. Hardly a best-seller, I would have thought, but the Boss went in with all guns blazing.

At a dinner in June in Warsaw attended by the general's chief speech writer, an army major, Cap'n Bob was reported in *The Times* to have pledged that Mirror Group Newspapers would give less coverage to the banned Solidarity movement in future.

His listeners were a trifle bewildered when they heard him declare his abiding support for Mrs Thatcher, while still being a committed Socialist and Labour Party member. Adding the additional advice that his hosts should apply BPC's unbeatable formula to the Polish economy.

'What is that, Mr Maxwell?' one curious official, unable to contain himself, inquired.

'What we have been doing, and I think I can say with some success,' the Boss told him, 'is buying up bankrupt printing companies. Rather like your factories.

'Then we say to the work force: "Look, we need 4,000 redundancies – take it or leave it. If you don't like it, we won't touch the place, and you'll have 12,000 out of work."

'There's always a bit of argy-bargy. But eventually everyone sees the logic of that, including the unions. So they take it. That's the way to do it.'

The Communist big-wigs around the table nodded vigorously. They saw the logic too.

At the end of his speech, even the Cap'n came close to stepping over the mark. He boasted of his friends in the Politburo in Moscow who entertained him in their country dachas. Adding jovially, as he sat down: 'Oh, and I'm thinking of appointing General Jaruzelski as the *Mirror*'s defence correspondent. Good idea?'

This time the heads did not react with such enthusiasm. Even if they did see some logic in that, too. All the same, they gave him a standing ovation.

Back home, someone in the news room looked out the cuttings on 'Poland – Political'. And found the last *Mirror* leader written on the country, dated September 1983.

'The human rights that Solidarity has demanded are those which British miners have enjoyed for generations. Poland is about as Socialist as East Germany is Democratic. It is under the Soviet Communist thumb. It is under harsh military rule. It is under the constant threat of Soviet invasion if it gets out of line.'

That was only two years before Cap'n Bob came in on the act. Isn't it amazing, what can happen in two years?

Now outrage followed, with Solidarity leaders jumping about like fleas, *Mirror* journalists condemned him for suggesting such a policy without consulting them, and Bob himself finally penned a letter to *The Times*.

'Mendacity is no stranger to *The Times* . . . But for the record, the conversation in the terms you described did not take place . . . ' He sounded like *Disgusted of Tunbridge Wells*.

So this was the background against which I flew in to record the great event.

General Jaruzelski was a small, balding man with dark, darting eyes hidden behind shaded glasses, and that was exactly how I saw him. Shifty is the word. You never knew where those eyes were looking, or the thoughts that were going on behind them.

In Maxwell's presence, the pair looked like Little and Large, and I always tried to tone down the contrast in size by photographing them from the correct angles, usually with the Polish leader closer to the camera.

I was given my usual 12 hours' notice. 'Mike, this is a particularly important occasion to me,' boomed the Boss after summoning me to his office. 'It's a big military event, and I'm expected to attend.'

With Poland's General Jaruzelski.

There was one immediate problem. Military meant uniforms. But unfortunately the old army uniform of Captain Robert Maxwell MC was no longer to hand. If it had been, I thought, it would have been interesting to see how the bulk of Cap'n Bob could be shoe-horned into it anyway.

The Boss solved that problem with his usual acumen – by having a fresh uniform specially made up for him by his personal Savile Row tailor, complete with shining Sam Browne belt and gleaming buckles, plus three officer's pips on the epaulettes. The maroon and white ribbon of the Military Cross blazed proudly from his left chest above two more rows of colourful decorations.

Next day we were on our way to Poland aboard Gulfstream 2. Next day being Friday, 1 September.

Leaving it to the last minute as usual, we soared into the summer skies from Heathrow at 8.30 a.m. – on the very day of the parade, which was due to start at 8.00 p.m. that evening in the famous Victoria Square, which I suppose can be classed as Warsaw's answer to our own Parliament Square.

Halfway into the flight, the Boss summoned me up front to sit next to him. Carina, the stewardess, poured us each a healthy slug of Stolichnaya, his favourite vodka, 52 per cent proof, with a tray of Beluga caviar to help us through the flight.

He downed the ice-cold drink in one, and waved his glass impatiently for a

In wartime uniform.

refill. Then he looked across the aisle at me. 'You will understand why this picture is so important, Mike, and why it will be one of the most important pictures of your career,' the Boss declared.

'Er, well . . .'

Actually, I had no idea but did I sense a threat that if I *didn't* get the picture, whatever it was, my career would be – well, retarded?

I summoned a look of intelligent inquiry.

'You will be photographing two very famous soldiers.'

Ah, now I knew.

I had already been briefed back in Holborn that Field Marshal Lord Bramall was the military VIP guest of honour representing the British Armed Services. It would make a good picture, the Field Marshal standing with General Jaruzelski by the War Memorial, the emotive equivalent of our Cenotaph, in the centre of the square.

'Right, R.M. Leave it all to me!'

Yes, I could get a poignant picture of two famous old war horses. Mentally I began setting it up.

Back in my seat I mulled over the schedule. We always stayed in the Victoria Hotel overlooking the square, and if I was lucky I would have a room looking out on to the action. The Victoria is Warsaw's most famous hotel, and certainly its most expensive.

There would be more than 50 countries represented, with delegates flying in from all over the world – from as far afield as America and Australia. They would be numbered in small groups in the square, and would stand there waiting to be called. Then they would proceed in a slow march across the 100 yards of cobbled square it would take them to reach the floodlit stone finger of the obelisk pointing into the evening sky.

Even from the schedule, I could see that it would be extremely impressive, and a real tear-jerker too.

We were due on parade at 7.30 p.m., half an hour before the actual ceremony began.

I am no more and no less interested in politics than the next man in the street. But riding the political gravy train with Robert Maxwell on the footplate, stoking the fires *and* gripping the controls, I figured it was prudent for me to find out about the various world figures I would be meeting.

I knew Poland was in a sorry state, and I had seen the bread queues for myself. Pure drinking water was at a premium, and toilet rolls were deemed a luxury.

For some, those were the days of wine, roses, Glasnost and Perestroika. But a cartoon in *The Times* two months before had shown General Jaruzelski

Cap'n Bob, trouserless, but doing the business.

dancing like a puppet on the strings of the puppet master – a Soviet hammer and sickle.

It had followed a Sunday election when the Polish Government had called on Lech Walesa's Solidarity party to join it in a coalition. And though only 62 per cent of the electorate had turned out to vote, it showed that it was unequivocally behind the unions and despised the government.

Into this maelstrom of political turmoil, Cap'n Bob entered with panache.

I sat with him in the shiny black limousine that had been waiting for us at the airport, as we passed through a grim Orwellian landscape of drab streets and houses that looked like bomb shelters.

'I am about to meet my old friend Jaruzelski,' Bob said, staring out of the window next to me. 'Do you know what some people are calling it? Fusion with a corpse!'

He was quoting Georges Clemenceau, the French statesman whose argumentative manner earned him the nickname of 'The Tiger' and whose style Maxwell rather liked.

He paused, and his face suddenly changed. For a moment – did I imagine it? – I thought I detected an expression of aching sadness behind the familiar bullish facade. Then the moment was gone, and maybe I hadn't seen anything after all.

But he was saying: 'Do you know how all this began, Mike?' He waved his

Spymaster to base . . . ?

Little and Large!

big hand at the window, embracing past and present. 'They found a murdered soldier in Polish uniform dumped in the grounds of the German radio transmitter in Upper Silesia. A place called Gleiwitz.

'It was left there as so-called evidence to the world that there had been a Polish attack on the sovereign territory of the Third Reich. It was classed as an act of aggression – though personally I believe it was probably some petty thief the Germans killed and put into a stolen uniform.

'But the Germans were able to call it an "act of aggression" against the Fatherland. The date was 31 August 1939. Next morning the tanks went in. And that's why we're here today.'

The Boss knew his history. I could listen to him for hours as he expounded his theories, took me through war and peace, rewriting the boundaries of the world map with the precision of an academic as conflicts came and went across the surface of our troubled planet. Cap'n Bob had a global view, no doubt about it.

Today Gleiwitz has become Gliwice, part of the historic Germany given over to Poland by the British, Americans and Russians at the Potsdam Conference in 1945.

We passed the graves of Polish soldiers that fill cemeteries throughout the bloodstained battlegrounds of World War II, most of them kept meticulously neat and many garnished with small bunches of flowers for the fallen.

Maybe it was Bob – possibly even Jaruzelski himself in one of our informal chats at a party or a reception – who had told me of the Polish cemeteries you can find today in Britain, France, Belgium, Holland, Germany, Italy, and stretching all the way across the Middle East to Libya and Egypt, and on into Iran, Iraq and Russia itself – the country that had so cruelly betrayed them in their hour of need in the Warsaw uprising.

That uprising by the Polish Home Army in 1944, as the world knows, lasted a magnificent 63 days. During that time the Old City was razed block by block, and a quarter of a million citizens died while Stalin infamously halted the Red Army across the river until the SS had completed their task.

But this time we were commemorating the first unspeakable act, the rape of an entire country. Our limousine nosed through sparse traffic towards the heart of the Old City, and I was glad to notice how busy the streets were, bustling with young people and shoppers – despite the obvious poverty and knowing that the currency was hopelessly devaluing by the week.

'The route the Wehrmacht's 30th Division took,' the Chairman murmured, still staring at the grey buildings passing by. 'Strange, when you think of it, Mike.'

'What is, R.M.?'

'The war began with one murder, and ended after the murder of millions more.'

He lapsed into thoughtful silence, and didn't speak again until we reached our hotel.

At 6.30 p.m. we mustered in the Presidential Suite for gin and tonic. For once, no vodka and no champagne.

Why? Because a uniformed figure was part of the group, a central, authoritative figure with various acolytes buzzing around him like bees round the proverbial honey-pot.

I recognised the elderly, ramrod-straight frame of Lord Bramall, and realised that the Cap'n had decided we were back in the Colonies. Which meant g and t all round.

There was no sign of Bob.

His Lordship and I shook hands. We had met before, and as usual the conversation immediately turned to cricket. 'I've forgotten,' said the old soldier. 'Which county is it that you support?'

'Lincolnshire, sir,' I told him.

'Oh, Minor Counties,' he said. 'Pity!'

'I've worked out where I'll be asking you to stand for the pictures, sir,' I pursued enthusiastically. 'The General will be standing ten feet from the memorial, with you on his left . . . '

'General?' The old warrior's brows knitted. 'I thought Maxwell was a captain!'

That's when it dawned on me.

Two very famous soldiers. With Jaruzelski not even in the frame.

At which moment the bedroom door opened, and out marched Captain Robert Maxwell MC, resplendent in his brand new uniform.

'How do I look?' he boomed, casting a general look about him that took in the whole room.

There were murmurs of approval all round.

The Cap'n beamed.

Then, to me: 'Well, Mike, have you worked out where you'll take the photographs?'

Well, up to that moment I thought I had. Quick change of battle plans needed. *Now* I knew why that picture was so important. And to my career, too. It also occurred to me that the Boss was trying to ingratiate himself into the Field Marshal's favour for reasons known only to himself.

'I've found the perfect spot, Chairman.'

'Good –'

'At the cenotaph.'

He broke in. 'Ah, when we are laying our wreaths. Excellent.' He turned to the Field Marshal. 'I told you this boy's good!'

Back to me. 'That's the picture I want.'

And that meant it was the picture I had to get.

At which point, unbeknown to any of us, we were on the fringe of drama and disaster! At least, I was.

The door opened, and an officious-looking functionary sporting a pallid complexion and a charcoal-grey suit entered.

Maxwell greeted him briskly. 'Come in. Have a drink.' Papers rustled. Gin and tonic appeared. The Polish official talked. The Captain and the Field Marshal listened intently, nodding from time to time.

As per the schedule, they would both be parading side by side in slow march through the throng of international delegates in the floodlit square, bearing wreaths to lay at the foot of the cenotaph.

An officer of the Polish army would take the wreaths from them, whereupon they would salute the fallen and retreat back to their place.

'Your number, gentlemen, is 36. You will find them painted on white boards in the appropriate place in the square.'

The three of them got up, all smiles. On the way to the door, the official paused. 'Oh, and by the way Captain Maxwell – you realise there are no photographic facilities at the memorial. No photographs are allowed.'

Oops! But then I remembered that at the Cenotaph in London no one gets close, either.

The door closed. In the silence that followed I watched Bob's complexion change from jovial pink to incandescent purple. But I could also see him controlling his fury, just, because of present company.

I have to say that with all his bombastic bravado – when it came to a *fait accompli* the Chairman knew when to call it a day, and not to waste his energies any more.

He looked at me, and shrugged his huge shoulders. And used one of his favourite terms. 'Bollocks!' – half to himself, but the whole room heard it.

It is one hour later, and we are congregated behind a rope barrier. The Maxwell entourage, myself included, watch as Captain Bob and Field Marshal Bramall march down the steps of the hotel and take up their appointed positions at Location Point 36. I notice that the Captain has added a cane and brown gloves to his wardrobe.

The square is abuzz with feverish activity. Spotlights from the rooftops pierce the gathering gloom, lighting up the scene, turning night into day.

Crowds surge forward, but quietly and with respect, pressing for a glimpse of the famous, held back by sweating uniformed police. It is uncannily like a West End movie premiere, only silent.

In the front row behind the thick golden cord, I can feel the pressure of bodies building up behind me.

Somewhere up there by the cenotaph 100 yards away, a military band is playing Elgar's *Enigma Variations*. The atmosphere is powerful and moving.

Pomp and circumstance reign.

Like the animals going into the Ark, the delegates are summoned in pairs, two by two, to pay their respects to the fallen.

Thirty . . . thirty-one . . . thirty-two . . .

An enormous wreath appears from nowhere, pressed into Bob's hand.

Thirty-four . . . thirty-five . . .

That's when I jump over the rope.

As the Captain, immaculate in khaki, and the equally elegant Lord Bramall move forward, I am suddenly there too. Squeezing between them, my blue mackintosh standing out between the two uniforms like ham in a sandwich, or at least a blue cheese sandwich.

Surprise!

Well, they are. And so is everybody else.

Slowly we pace in a solemn goose-step, shoulder to shoulder, feet rising rhythmically with measured tread. Bob on my left, Bramall on my right.

Left . . . right . . .

Left . . . right . . .

The Captain shoots me a sideways glance, a mixture of astonishment and (I hope) admiration at my cheek.

'Ah, Michael!' The voice is heavy, but not displeased. 'There you are!'

Left . . . right . . .

Left . . . right . . .

We are in perfect time, boots ringing on cold stone cobbles.

'Yes, R.M., and this is what we'll do –' I keep talking, while staring straight ahead.

A camera is tucked inside my raincoat. Around us, thousands are watching in respectful silence. All the time I am waiting for a hand to grab my collar as we pace the long road down to the waiting obelisk, magnificently floodlit in the distance.

Left . . . right . . .

'I know how we'll get this, Chairman!'

They are both listening.

'Go on!'

'When you salute –' I fill in the details.

We approach the cenotaph.

A uniformed Polish officer reaches for the wreaths. As he turns his back I keep going, over a white line, ahead of them both. And I turn with a smart pirouette, grabbing my Leica, whipping it out from under my raincoat.

'Now!'

Their hands rise in unison, in stiff salute.

Back in uniform.

Flash!

One frame only, but it is enough.

The interloper scuttles to catch up as the pair goose-step solemnly back, and takes his place between them.

Left . . . right . . .

Left . . . right . . .

Captain Robert Maxwell MC bestows the ultimate accolade.
'Mister, you are a fucking genius!'

Next day, we are to fly in Gulfstream 2 heading not for London but onward to Gdansk. From the hotel, an hour before take-off, the Chairman phones through my new appointment to Head Office in Holborn – Chief Photographer, Mirror Group Newspapers – making it official.

Nice. Champagne will flow on the jet. The blue-eyed boy is on his way. Another commemoration of the anniversary of the invasion is scheduled for 2 September. Another parade, this time in the industrial town of Gdansk, home of Solidarity.

Bob is due to meet Lech Walesa, the Arthur Scargill of the Polish workers, a meeting which would be a wonderful photo opportunity. But at the

With Lech Walesa.

92

eleventh hour, a message comes through.

Sorry, no time to see the Boss. Pressure of work. No formal meeting possible.

As soon as the Old Man hears that, he decides not to put himself out. 'It would be a waste of my time,' he says, concealing his disappointment under a veneer of indifference. A pause. Then: 'Mike, you will go in my place!'

'Me, Chairman?'

'Yes, and take some photographs while you're about it, Mr Snapper.'

The newly appointed Maxwell emissary took off with the Boss in the private jet on the 40-minute hop to Gdansk. Even from the air, as we circled in for the landing, the place looked like a soulless dockland which managed to be depressing even on a sunny day.

A line-up of equally grey-faced union shipyard officials waited to greet us on the tarmac. No red carpet, but neither of us was expecting any.

I disembarked first, a lone photographer descending the steps with a hopeful smile and a bulging camera case.

But I got away with it, pleading the Chairman's apologies and pressure of work (hinting at international events) that precluded him from being there in person.

Maxwell headed for the hotel. I climbed into a waiting Lada and was driven to the shipyard. The parade there was, again, enormous. It reminded me of the British Legion, as ranks of aged figures wearing their uniforms and their medals marched with watery-eyed pride to a familiar obelisk on the waterfront by the docks to place their floral tributes to fallen comrades.

As an invited VIP, albeit by proxy, I had a privileged position by the memorial. I was close enough to spot the stocky figure of Lech Walesa surrounded by his coterie of acolytes standing at attention a few paces away.

Finally the ceremony was over. Lech was deep in conversation with his comrades. I took an inward breath, and strode purposefully towards him, without hindrance and extended the hand of *bonhomie*.

'Mr President!'

He looked up.

'My name is Mike Maloney. I am Mr Robert Maxwell's personal assistant, and may I offer you his best wishes. And may I say how sorry he is that you cannot meet him today.' A translator at his elbow conveyed my words.

On the basis of charisma, Maxwell versus Walesa – strictly no contest! As the Chairman's ambassador, I have to say that my immediate impression was of a small, burly man exuding neither humour nor warmth. Fred Flintstone could have taught him a few lessons in charm.

'I am so sorry,' Walesa said. 'I was looking forward to meeting Mr Axewell.'

Under the Grand Arch in Paris.

Axewell? That would be one that *Private Eye* would dearly love to have overheard.

'Can we not rectify this in some way?' he asked.

'Well,' said Mr Diplomat, thinking fast on his feet. 'There is a way. My Chairman is at the National Hotel, and I know he would be delighted if you could join us for drinks in his room.'

'Well, yes . . . I do need to meet him – '

Why, I never knew.

But two hours later, Lech Walesa was ushered into Bob's palatial room – or as palatial as you could get in Gdansk – to be greeted by the Chairman with a beaming smile and a hearty handshake.

And for me, another pat on the back as we left for home next day.

More foreign travel, this time a hop across the Channel to Paris. I should emphasise at this point that it was unwise – actually, suicidal – to correct the Boss. He was never, ever wrong.

We were driving together through the nostalgic streets, with a car load of dignitaries, when I recognised a particular house through the railings. 'Oh, look R.M.! Mrs Simpson's house!'

I had always been intrigued by Edward and his scandalous romance, and read every word I could about them. She must have been about 90.

'That's where she lives.'

'You mean that's where she *lived*. She's dead.'

Well, in fact she died two years later on 24 April 1986, but I couldn't correct him. No way was I going to say: 'No, R.M., you're wrong!' Particularly in company. No one else said anything, either.

So that day Mrs Simpson died two years ahead of her time. And Cap'n Bob, blissfully unaware, went about his business in the City of Dreams.

On to Madrid, in high summer, and an audience with King Juan Carlos of Spain. The Cap'n and I were staying at the Ritz, and he was in the mood for champagne.

The Ritz is a nice enough hotel, but they didn't stock the bubbly that the Boss wanted. 'Mike, go out and get some Crystal champagne!'

I went out into the hot afternoon streets of the city, and started searching. After half an hour I found a wine merchant that stocked it, and hadn't closed for the siesta. 'Si, señor! It is fifteen t'ousand pesetas a bottle.'

That sounded like a lot of pesetas, but in fact it worked out at £75. I settled for two bottles, paid by credit card – Maxwell never carried any money with him, not even a dime – and took them back to the hotel. There we proceeded

With King Juan Carlos of Spain.

to finish them off in his suite, as a warm-up to next day's meeting with Spanish royalty.

The king sent a limousine for us, and we travelled in style for the 90 minutes it took to get us to his country estate in the spectacular countryside outside Madrid. These are the mountains where Hollywood mogul Samuel Bronson filmed epics like *El Cid* and *The Fall of the Roman Empire*. Farther south, straight down as the crow flies all the way to Almeria, was where Spain was put on the movie map with Clint Eastwood and his Spaghetti Westerns.

The king's hideaway was an elegant hacienda set back from the road behind a high wall and with a lot of security. Juan Carlos, a charming man with a perfect command of English, greeted us courteously, and invited us into his equally elegant book-lined study.

Mr Snapper meets the King of Spain.

Over tea, they talked about printing. At times like this, Mr Snapper played gooseberry, seemingly attentive but in fact with his thoughts far away. The one thing I was *not* expected to do was to offer an opinion. *'Quite honestly, Bob, I don't think it's worth ten million!'* Tempting, though.

So I kept quiet, and tried to look interested. Occasionally the Boss would turn to me with a raised eyebrow and say: 'Right?' Whereupon I would nod knowingly, confirming whatever he had just been expounding.

Yes, I was a good listener. And I was never bored.

Wait, I tell a lie.

I was bored in East Berlin in the company of the East German leader Erich Honecker, after Bob and I had passed through the chilling Checkpoint Charlie to meet him at his office. Maxwell was there to discuss some book he was planning to publish – presumably in the *Wit and Wisdom* series – and all I

97

A wintry smile from East German leader Erich Honecker.

managed to tempt was a wintry smile out of the diminutive Honecker.

The only light spot I can recall in our trips through the drab highways and byways of Eastern Europe was a moment in Czechoslovakia, Bob's homeland, when he spotted three peasant women trudging along the road together. 'Stop the car!' he ordered, and wound down the window to engage the ladies in conversation in their own language.

Then he turned to me. 'Take a picture, Mike. These are our new Page Three girls! We'll show the *Sun* a thing or two!'

Dutifully, I obeyed my master's voice.

Otherwise I was bored in Bulgaria, where Bob was the proud recipient of the People's Republic *Order Stara Planina* (First Class). I was bored in

The Page Three girls

Czechoslovakia, at meetings with General Jaruzelski. I was bored in Hungary, where he took a major shareholding in the government's newspaper, *Magyar Hirlap*. And in Rumania, I was so bored I can't honestly remember what I was there for anyway.

Terminal *ennui* set in because I didn't speak the language, and if they weren't speaking English I hadn't the foggiest idea what was going on.

But I still remembered to nod.

CHAPTER SIX

All at Sea on the *Lady G.*

I fell in love with *Lady Ghislaine* on a balmy February night in 1988, with the moon riding high in a sky spangled with stars, and the temperature hovering at around 70 degrees. You will gather I was not in the UK.

Sleek, seductive, shapely – she was every red-blooded male's dream. I mean, how many men can boast a mistress who gives you a ten-day holiday worth a quarter of a million dollars, and supplies you with every creature comfort you could wish for and a few more besides?

That was the *Lady Ghislaine*, the luxury yacht that Cap'n Bob had bought for £15 million from Adnan Kashoggi's brother, and named after Bob's daughter.

'I need you on the yacht, Mike!' The familiar boom rang down the phone as I sat at my desk on one of those grey overcast days where damp and depression can seep into your very soul. I never did like winter, anyway.

'Where exactly is she R.M.?'

'St Martin.' The phone went dead.

The reason, as I learned five minutes later after hot-footing it up to the Ninth Floor, was simple. The Chairman wanted me to photograph his pride and joy for a glossy brochure. He was already planning to rent the *Lady G.* out to the rich and famous who felt in need of a breath of sea air – at $25,000 a day – and some had already sampled her.

I flew out, alone, on 18 February with an open-ended return ticket. First to Miami. Then the Yellowbird flight of Eastern Airlines down to St Martin in the Virgin Islands, which you'll find nestling mid-way along the spine of the Caribbean.

In the arrivals hall of the small, sleepy airport, a ship's officer in crisp white ducks and gold epaulettes was waiting. I introduced myself.

His name was Stephen, he was the First Officer, and I was aware of curious glances as he snapped into a smart salute. 'This way, sir.'

We walked outside, and the humid night air wrapped itself around me like a warm glove. My spirits rose. I always did have a hankering for the tropics, and my first impression of St Martin was reassuring. Tall, slender reeds waved a welcome by the roadside, and palm trees bent their green fronds in the soft, scented breeze, a breeze redolent of dusky maidens and rum punch.

'When is Mr Maxwell due?' asked the officer.

'I was rather hoping you could tell *me*. I'm afraid I've got no idea.'

'We never hear anything until the last minute,' he indicated a black stretch limousine, glaringly out of place among the battered taxis and scooters that seemed to make up the island's transport system.

'That's par for the course,' I said. Being on the Maxwell payroll meant being fast on your feet, and trying to second-guess the Old Man at every stage of the game.

A beautiful aerial shot of the yacht. (Aerophoto Schiphol B.V.)

'Then you've got the ship to yourself, sir.'

I could live with that.

Twenty minutes later we pulled up amid a cluster of derelict shacks and rundown jetties that passed for the main port. I looked out to sea – and caught my breath.

She was beautiful. An elegant white yacht decked from stem to stern in fairy lights that glowed like fireflies against the black ocean. There were other boats dotted around, but in the sunset the *Lady Ghislaine* stood out like a queen among a herd of commoners.

Talk about love at first sight!

The tender was waiting, a large motor launch with an open front and an enclosed cabin to protect the occupants from the elements.

Well, if it was inevitable, I figured I had better lie back and enjoy it.

Close to, she looked huge. Her vital statistics are impressive, too. Length: 180 feet. Tonnage: 430. Number of decks: four – 'unusual in a yacht of her size', as the brochure would eventually inform prospective customers. Cruising speed: 14 knots.

Plus, to quote the brochure, 'Experienced Crew of 13 comprising Captain, First Officer, Chief Engineer, Second Engineer, Chief Steward, wine steward, two stewardesses, chef and four deckhands'.

I climbed the sloping gangplank to an open door in the hull, to be piped aboard by one of the crew with a bosun's whistle. Long peep . . . short peep . . . long peep.

'Do you mind taking off your shoes, sir. Footwear is not allowed at any time on the yacht.'

'Certainly.' I had been warned about that already.

'This way, sir. Your cabin is ready for you.'

I had been looking forward to my first meeting with the *Lady G.* ever since Betty Maxwell had described their prized nautical possession to me over dinner one night in Headington Hill Hall, the Maxwell's country estate near Oxford. She had told me how Bob had surprised her – in fact, surprised the whole family – by taking them on a 'mystery tour' one weekend when they had been celebrating their son Ian's 30th birthday.

Bob had piled them all into the Gulfstream, and flown the family to Amsterdam. Followed by a drive to a secluded harbour 20 miles away – where this beautiful yacht lay at anchor by the quayside. A scaffolding had been erected at the bows, and a champagne bottle on its cord stood waiting.

Daughter Ghislaine did the honours, smashing the bottle against the side – just as a cloth was whipped away to reveal her own name in gold capitals on the hull.

The Cap'n with his pride and joy.

The interior of the ship apparently had been unfinished when Bob snapped it up, and Betty became a key figure in decorating it, along with designer Jon Bannenberg and his team.

For me, that decor meant a state room port-side for'ard on the lower deck, which would become my 'usual cabin'. I stepped over the threshold – and immediately my feet were lost in the white carpet. The pile, not to exaggerate, was at least two inches thick. My toes in their socks disappeared in two inches of soft fur.

I surveyed the surroundings with mounting satisfaction, tinged with disbelief.

First off, the four-poster bed. It could have slept three people. On the embroidered silk counterpane were laid out my togs for the duration of my stay, however long that would be. Crisp white shorts and a tennis shirt in cellophane bags, sparkling white canvas-soled deck shoes. All brand new and all to my size.

I remembered that when I picked up my air ticket from the Ninth Floor, they had checked me ahead from London. 'The yacht want your height, your weight, your shoe size.'

Already, the *Lady G.* was taking on a personality of her own!

'And also, if you're a vegetarian.'

Milady thinks of everything.

In addition, I found a towel robe hanging behind the door with the monogram LG inlaid in gold, plus a blue and gold toilet bag similarly embossed.

There was a bath and shower *en suite*. The tastefully matching curtains by the windows were worked by a bedside button, so I wouldn't even have to get out of bed to see where we'd moored in the mornings. Sofa. Television. Fresh flowers in the cabins every day. Even the aroma of the carpet combining with the mahogany woodwork smelled of unabashed wealth and luxury.

A knock at the door.

The steward outside, with a menu in his hand. 'What time would you like dinner, sir?'

Outside, through the window, the last glowing rays of the sun streaked the Caribbean sky crimson. Eight bells were approaching.

'Perhaps a drink before dinner?'

'Certainly, sir. We have already made a cocktail in your honour.'

The cocktail in my honour turned out to be a heady rum-based banana concoction, fine-tuned in a liquidiser and with a subtle, but lethal kick. It was courtesy of Jeremy the barman, a figure I would get to know well over the ensuing days.

'It's a Yellowbird, sir.'

Like the plane. 'Seems to be a popular name around these parts,' I said.

Wandering through the main lounge with my drink in deep, carpeted silence, I spotted the visitors' book on a desk. I signed my name with a flourish.

Why not? I was a visitor, after all. Then I saw the name immediately above mine.

Francis Albert Sinatra.

'Yes, Mike, he was here last month.' Captain Mike Insull – the name Mike figured large in R.M.'s life – was a tall, dark-haired professional with an affable demeanour concealing a lifetime at sea. He had joined me in the lounge for a courtesy drink, though afterwards I would find myself always eating alone.

'Frank Sinatra?'

'None other. Dino was with him.'

'Dean Martin – '

'Sure enough. We piped them aboard. I saluted, and said: "Welcome to the *Lady Ghislaine*, sir. My name is Captain Insull."

'To which he replied: "My name is Sinatra. And where is the bar?"'

Other signatures in the burgundy leather-bound book I noticed belonged to Roger Moore, Michael Caine and his wife Shakira, and Kirk Kerkorian, the legendary Hollywood mogul, financier and friend of Howard Hughes.

Over the heady months to come, names of the rich, famous and powerful would jostle for space in those pages.

Right now, floating serenely at anchor half a mile out in the moonlit bay, the *Lady Ghislaine* awaited her Master's pleasure. Except that the Master wasn't there, but I was.

I had changed for dinner into natty navy-blue blazer and white flannels, as befits the temporary sole occupant of a luxury yacht. Now I made the most of it.

I did some swift mental arithmetic. If Sinatra had been paying $25,000 a day just for stepping aboard, and I would be there, say, ten days – that was a quarter-million dollars worth of holiday for yours truly.

Yes, I could certainly live with that.

A spot of music was called for. Vivaldi's *Four Seasons* flowed from a console, filling the room. Satellite phones (at seven pounds a minute) were available. First call was to my Mum in Lincoln.

'Are you all right, son? Are you enjoying yourself?'

'Struggling, Mum. But I'll get over it.' I had moved on to Dom Perignon, and lifted a glass to toast frozen England and absent friends.

'Just don't work too hard, son.'

'I won't, Mum. Promise!'

I was feeling peckish. 'I'll take dinner now.' Down a spiral staircase, where another vista opened out – the incredible luxury of the *Ghislaine* dining-room.

A long glass-topped mahogany table that seats 16, but now there was just one place laid – for me.

The ceiling was mirrored, and the walls too. Further exploration would show that virtually every surface on the ship seemed to have a mirror on it. Everywhere you looked, your face stared back at you from some corner or other.

That was how Bob found the decor, possibly as a reflection of Arab narcissism, and mostly he left it that way. Sometimes I would be faced with the unnerving sight of five Cap'n Bobs bearing down on me – and once I even captured it on camera, much to his amusement.

I sat down at the head of the table, and in the deathly hush took in the surroundings. A steward and two stewardesses stood immobile at attention, ready to respond to my every call.

I noticed the glasses: finest leaded crystal, cushioned in a concealed cabinet set into the mahogany panelling. The china was Royal Doulton.

I had chosen Beluga caviar and Lobster Thermidor for my first-ever meal on Milady *Ghislaine*. Start as you intend to continue seemed the best motto. I would order another favourite, Boeuf Wellington, for lunch tomorrow.

Every day, a different menu would be available. The system was to order lunch at breakfast and order dinner at lunchtime.

For wine, I would direct my attentions to the Lafittes or the Margaux reds. For white, Chablis *Premier Cru* was the house wine, and I could add Mersault or Montigny if my taste buds were in the mood. Sixty bottles nestled in a huge rack located below the stairs. The steward would take me over, and I would choose the wines I wanted.

But that first night, I saw for the first time the down side of being a surrogate millionaire on your own yacht. The dark side of what should surely be a full, rose-coloured moon. Say hello again to the Lonely Man!

The message that comes over, loud and clear, is that: it can be a solitary life. First off, what do you say to the staff? What do they say to you?

After a few polite 'Yes sirs, no sirs', the dining-room lapsed into silence while the three of them stood there watching me, and I listened to the sound of my own jaws chomping on the lobster.

Unnerving, almost surreal – and I suspected that a long week stretched ahead. Well, I'd just have to learn to live with it.

But where was the Chairman? There was no word from London. Captain Insull just shrugged and shook his head when I raised an eyebrow in an unspoken query.

So I got on with the job I was there for, and photographed that ship from stem to stern. I don't think I missed a foot.

Let me give you the brief guided tour.

I detected a definite pecking order about the *Lady G.*, inherited from her previous Arab owners.

For a start, the sitting-room – grandly known as the International Observation Lounge. As I snapped away, I realised how the three tiers, curved like a football stadium, implied a strict code of position and distinction. Owners and VIPs on the top tier, minions at the bottom.

The lounge with its restful apple-white decor had a panoramic window

Kevin and Ian with the Lady G.

for'ard with a sweeping 180-degree view around the ship.

More interesting, there was a glass-bottomed jacuzzi perched immediately above the aft lounge. This enabled anyone sitting below to get a worm's-eye – as distinct from bird's-eye – view of the posteriors of those cavorting in the jacuzzi. Show time! It's all happening up there!

Betty in fact had replaced most of the glass with solid wood panelling, leaving just a small circle through which watery light filtered down to the lounge.

Mrs Maxwell had her own state room on the same deck as mine. Bob had decided to call his the Owner's Suite, located on the middle deck, with direct access to the after deck where he would meet his final date with destiny.

Inside the Owner's Suite, I set up my tripod, worked out the lighting, and began with the vast king-size bed that could accommodate even the Cap'n's enormous bulk – by now a conservative 18 stone, and rising.

The bed had His 'n' Her bathrooms on either side, plus a large dressing-room, and an incredible array of hi-tech gadgetry. Four remote-control hand sets could be operated from the bed, connecting variously with satellite TV, video, a CD player and the quadrophonic sound system.

Bob, I would discover, always wore a striped night-shirt aboard the *Lady G.*, plus a conical sleeping cap with a pom-pom. For conical, read comical – but I somehow managed to keep a straight face if I saw him wearing it.

And, sorry, there's no photo of that eyesore for sore eyes. I wish. I wish . . .

The next few days trundled by like a slow locomotive going nowhere. The routine became positively soporific. My photos were in the can, but I had no word from London and no desire to rush back to wintry Britain.

Instead, I began my exhausting schedule with breakfast on the deck, aft. Coffee and croissants would be the order of the day, with magnificent fresh fruits of guava and papaya served in a basket by one of the stewardesses. And still I always ate alone, every single meal.

The one room on the entire ship where Cap'n Bob never set foot was the gymnasium on the upper deck. Me, I spent an hour in there every day, limbering up on the keep-fit bike, swinging weights, lifting bars. Thirty minutes in the morning, ditto in the evening.

Paradise lasted five days. In that time I think I came dangeorusly close to melt-down. All I had to do was snap my fingers – and it happened.

'I think I feel like a stroll.'

'Certainly, sir. The launch will take you ashore. Which island would you like to visit today?'

'How about Anguilla?'

Anguilla it is.

I took a two-way walkie-talkie with me, beamed into the *Lady G.*'s radio room. I would stroll on the white sands of a beach, browse through a local paper, sunbathe, perhaps find a fish restaurant for a spot of lunch.

When I wanted to get back on board, I'd call up the yacht.

'Can you send the launch?'

'Right away, sir.'

And right away it was.

I would also ask: 'Any messages for me?'

'No, sir.'

All dreams come to an end, and on Fantasy Island it was finally time for the real world to bite back.

On the sixth day an air of tension suddenly pervaded the ship. The word came through via the radio room: *The Old Man's on his way!*

That evening, at sunset, I leaned over the rail and watched his massive bulk on the tender looming out of the dusk. Subtly, the ship's atmosphere had

Betty gets to grips with Bob.

already changed. Everyone was on red alert.

He greeted me jovially, and I was pleased to see Betty was with him. 'How are you doing, Mr Snapper?'

Mr Snapper was doing very well, thank you Chief.

'Good. What's for dinner?'

That night, at a dining table set for three, I regaled them with the Wild Boar story, which had become the stuff of legend in Fleet Street.

It goes like this. At a Labour Party Conference in Blackpool, Mike Molloy (yet another Mike on the cast list) was Editor of the *Daily Mirror*. One of the senior Maxwell executives was a chap named Neil Bentley – who, you may recall, had been dubbed Mr Crapper in one of the Chairman's lighter moments on our jaunt to Khartoum. Neil was a large, jovial fellow topping six foot four and weighing the scales at about 20 stone – in physique more than a match for the Old Man.

He had taken it upon himself to supply Maxwell with his nightly repast, and was always asking Molloy what he thought Cap'n Bob would like for dinner. I was there when finally, in exasperation, Molloy declared: 'Oh, I think he'll fancy wild boar tonight!'

That did it. Bentley spent the whole of the next day ringing every conceivable type of restaurant and butcher throughout the length and breadth of the land to try and snare a wild boar.

And – wonder of wonders! – he found one.

In Aberdeen.

Don't ask me how, but he did it. At enormous cost, the porcine carcass was driven at high speed from Aberdeen to Blackpool, and delivered to the hotel. With instructions for it to be served up for dinner that night, complete with apple in mouth.

I was chatting to Molloy in the hotel lobby when a beaming Bentley appeared breathlessly at his elbow. To inform him: 'We've done it. The pig is here!'

Only to be told by Molloy that the Old Man had changed his mind. 'He doesn't want pork. He's having fish!'

It was all a wind-up, of course.

Cap'n Bob knew nothing of the story – until I told him that night over dinner on the *Lady G*.

His bellows of laughter filled the quiet Caribbean night, floating out through the open windows across the bay.

Finally he wiped his eyes with his napkin.

'That's a very funny story, Mike. Now tell it again.'

'What – ?'

'I want to hear it again.'

And the snapper turned raconteur went through the same script all over again.

In all, I would stay ten days enjoying my first flirtation with that beautiful ship. Betty Maxwell left for America after only two days, leaving Bob and myself together for three more before my time was up and I was ordered back to base.

Ironically, next door to the gymnasium where I worked out every day, was a no-go area for everyone – except by direct invitation. That meant both guests and crew.

This was the open private deck where Bob, with his satellite phone at his

Taking a dip.

elbow, sat enfolded into a white leather seat and relaxed by himself.

Or, sometimes, with company.

The day after Betty left, it was almost too hot to move. I was reclining in a deck-chair at the stern reading a paperback, brain happily in neutral, when a crew member rushed up to me. His face was ashen.

'Mike, quick, you've got to help me!'

I dropped my book. 'What on earth's the matter?'

'I don't know what to do.'

'What's the matter?' I repeated.

'I've just seen something awful. I knocked on the door to the Chairman's private sun lounge, and walked in. I could hear classical music being played, so maybe that's why he didn't hear my knock.'

'And – ' I prompted.

'Well – there he was. I mean, I caught him in the act! Actually, you know,

Relaxing on board with the Cap'n, Jean and Betty.

doing it. He was sitting in his chair with this girl kneeling on the deck in front of him–'

'All right,' I said. 'I get the picture.' I believe it is known as *flagrante delicto*, but somehow I felt that now wasn't the time for semantics. The poor chap was genuinely shaken.

'And then – ?' I pursued.

'I just turned and shot out.'

Very wise. 'Did he see you?'

'I think his mind was on other things, sir.'

'I don't suppose he was listening to Ravel's *Bolero* by any chance?' I tried to lighten the mood.

'What shall I do?'

'Nothing,' I said. 'Don't worry about it. Just forget you saw anything – and don't say a word to anyone else.'

Neither of us spoke about it again. My own feeling was more of surprise than anything else. How on earth had the Old Man smuggled the girl on board? I never even got a sighting of her.

In the main lounge, the sextagonal carpet in the centre could be peeled back to

Relaxing on the deck of the Lady Ghislaine *(Picture by Betty Maxwell)* . . .

display a dance floor. Bob's own home-grown disco! On one side, a panel covered a complete music console like a roll-top desk. In the evenings I happily took charge as resident MC and DJ combined, choosing the music

. . . but still in contact with base camp (picture by Betty Maxwell).

that would filter through the ship.

Mostly it was classical. Both Bob and Betty liked Vivaldi, Mozart, Chopin, Strauss, Mahler – and no head-banging heavy metal allowed. There must have been 600 CDs on the ship.

And above us, a similar panel in the leather-padded ceiling came away to reveal a battery of disco lights. Again, yours truly was in charge of making things hum when the occasion called for it. As it did on Betty's last night aboard ship.

'Goodnight, Bob. Goodnight, Mike.' She gave him a kiss on the cheek. 'I shall retire.' It wasn't late, around 11 p.m., but she had a full day ahead and wanted an early night.

Off she went to her own cabin, leaving the two of us together. I popped outside to smoke one of Bob's finest Havanas – no smoking was allowed below deck – and was feeling drowsily content.

Every one of the four reception rooms on the *Lady Ghislaine* housed a large humidor, complete with unusual ignitors – ten-inch silver sticks with a switch on the side. A tongue of flame shot out when you pressed it.

As a cigar man myself, I was instrumental in introducing the Cap'n to Fidel Castro's favourite weed – the famous *Cohiba*, a massive seven-inch torpedo-shaped cheroot that would change hands back home in London at a grotesque £20 a time. Bob poured his own DP '82 vintage from the ice bucket. That was one thing the *Lady G.* was never short of: chilled champagne and wine. In fact, there was a refrigerator in all the connecting rooms on the upper deck, loaded with his favourites and outside the main lounge, no fewer than three fridges side by side.

He slumped back in his armchair, saying nothing, lost in his own thoughts. I knew better than to interrupt them and was happy to float along on a heady cloud of Mozart.

Suddenly the phone rang, shattering the atmosphere like a stone through a window. The Chairman shook himself awake, and lumbered off to take it in his study.

The call lasted 15 minutes – and when he came back, he was a changed man. 'I've fried another big fish, Mike. Now – let's liven this place up!'

Inexplicably, he starts to shuffle around the room, snapping his fingers. Suddenly I am in the presence of Zorba the Greek.

'What about Mrs M., Bob?'

'Don't worry about her!'

'All right, then – ' I pull back the carpet, and head for the console. Switch the CD to a tape, and the soothing strains of Mozart's *Symphonie No 36* in C Major change abruptly into *I'm Her Yesterday Man*, with Chris Andrews in full voice.

'Ah, the Beatles!' The Boss was always eager to demonstrate his knowledge on every subject.

Behind the console, I flick switches. Lights, action – but for once, no camera! Above us the disco lights flash on. The elegant lounge is transformed into an instant discotheque – with Cap'n Bob taking the floor.

Off with his jacket. In open-neck shirt, the Boss shuffles around with renewed vigour. I get into the mood. If Bob is Zorba, I'll be Alan Bates. The pair of us move around the small floor facing each other, Bob waving his hands in the air like a soccer supporter on the terraces, fingers snapping like castanets.

I start to sing in time with Chris Andrews.

'I'm her yesterday man . . . Well, my friend, that's what I am . . . that's what I am . . .'

'I never knew you could sing, Mike . . .'

Finally his huge bulk heads towards the spiral staircase to his bedroom. Party time is finished.

Over his shoulder, the sonorous voice floats back.

'Stick to taking pictures, Mr Snapper!'

And a deep chuckle follows him out of the door.

Not for the first time, he hasn't even said goodnight.

8 June 1990. A Friday evening. I was in my office BMW heading up the A11 to Norfolk to deliver a lecture on photo-journalism to a convention of camera clubs in Norwich.

The BMW – I felt the Roller would be a bit showy – was purring along at a comfortable 70, when the car phone rang.

'Mike, where are you?' the Boss's voice boomed in my ear.

'In Norfolk, R.M. I'm halfway to Norwich.' It was rare for him to ring me personally. Normally he got his secretary to do it, so it must be important.

The heavy voice rumbled out of the phone. 'I need you in Cannes for the launch of the *European*. On the boat. By tomorrow morning, 11 o'clock sharp, just for the day. I want you to direct the video of the occasion. The President of France will be there. All right?'

'Well – not really, R.M.,' I replied hesitantly.

'Why not, Mister?'

Uh-oh. Mister was bad news. I tried to explain.

'I'm guest of honour at a camera club convention, and I have to make a speech after the dinner. I can't let them down – and it won't be easy for me to drive all the way to Heathrow afterwards.'

'Ah,' he said. 'I accept that.' Inwardly I sighed with relief. It meant I was off the hook.

But not quite.

'You realise this is one of the most important functions you'll ever attend in your life?'

Well, I hadn't. And, quite honestly, I wasn't sure it was going to be.

'What if I send my helicopter for you?'

'Oh! Well – '

'That's settled, then. Can we land it in Norfolk?'

'I don't know, R.M. But I can find out.'

'You do that.' The phone went dead.

I called up Captain Dick Cowley at Mirror Group Newspapers in his private apartment in Orbit House where he lived with his wife. Dick was always on stand-by across the street from Maxwell House, so that he could get to the helicopter pad in minutes.

Captain Cowley answered.

I told him: 'Dick, the Old Man wants the chopper to land in Norfolk tomorrow to pick me up. I've got to get to Cannes. Can you do it?'

'Norfolk?' His Aussie accent came loud and clear down the line. 'Where's that?'

'In East Anglia. You'll find it on the map,' I said wearily. 'There's a school I know . . . '

Seven a.m. next morning The dinner had been a great success, which was why I was nursing a hangover. I drove to the school playing field, to find the red-white-and-blue outline of the Maxwell helicopter already there, squatting on the grass like a giant mosquito. No one seemed to have complained, or rung the police.

I left my car at the gates, hurried across and clambered aboard.

Ninety minutes later the Maxwell chopper whirred out of the sky into

Charles de Gaulle Airport outside Paris, where the Maxwell Gulfstream 2 (call sign VR-BOB) was warming up on the apron immediately next to the bull's-eye landing pad.

Apart from the crew of three, I was the only passenger. Mentally I started to tot up the cost – from a helicopter landing in Norfolk to a private jet landing in Nice. *Sacre bleu!* I lost count. And it wasn't over yet.

Amid the floral splendour of Nice Airport, with the early sun slanting its special light – a photographer's dream – into the arrival hall, a uniformed figure stood with a cardboard sign bearing my name on it. Spelled *Moloney*, wrong as usual.

I headed for the Rolls-Royce parked outside.

All I had with me was my usual green overnight holdall – plus my ever-present Leica camera. But it was enough for a day trip to the Riviera.

On the jetty in the Old Harbour at Cannes, Captain Mike Insull was waiting in person to take me out to sea on the ship's tender, dressed all in the familiar white, with the ship's crest on his shirt.

He greeted me affably. 'This is going to be some party, Mike,' he said. 'I thought I should warn you.'

And so it proved.

I was spot on time, and actually boarded the *Lady Ghislaine* with ten minutes to spare from the appointed hour. The first thing I did was to take my shoes off – just as each of the 300 guests would have to do when they arrived.

A three-camera crew stood at the stern, shifting their feet, waiting to be briefed. 'Make sure you get the important people, and cover everything and everybody,' I ordered.

The important people included Credit Lyonnaise officials, top brass from other French business houses, and a smattering of showbiz glitterati including our own Julie Walters.

The guests began to arrive. All of them, from President François Mitterand downwards, shuffled around in their socks or stockinged feet – and I couldn't help noticing the French Premier wore natty nylon socks.

Bright idea! I would direct my camera team to film the guests at ankle level – a piece of footage that the Chairman later would describe as 'inspired'.

Bully for Mr Snapper!

The party, awash with the inevitable Dom Perignon, began. Tables on the stern deck were groaning under the weight of tubs of the finest Beluga caviar (at £250 a tub), smoked salmon and lobster claws.

I prowled the decks with my camera. Photographed Cap'n Bob with his star guest. President Mitterand – recognising me from past encounters – threw me an amiable grin: 'Ah, Bob, I see your young man is in action again!'

With French President François Mitterand.

To which the Boss responded jovially: 'Of course. That's what I pay him for.'

Three hours later. As the last guest floated off in the tender on a sea of champagne and euphoria, Maxwell heaved a deep sigh of satisfaction. He put a large hand round my shoulder.

'Didn't that go well?' he declared.

For *me*, yes it had. And for the launch of the *European* too. It looked like another Maxwell venture was up and running.

Eighty bottles of Dom Perignon had been quaffed that day, and I had done my share of the quaffing. I had also played my part in celebrating the big event by stuffing myself with spoonfuls of best Beluga and as many lobster claws as I could find. So had the Chairman. The only difference, I couldn't help noticing, being that Cap'n Bob ate the claws, too.

Suddenly at my elbow, he boomed: 'Let's have some lunch, Mike. But first I've got to ring London. You go to the dining-room and help yourself to whatever you like.'

Oh magic, foolish words! Three waiters in white tuxedos and matching socks were hovering. I had worked hard. Now I was in the mood.

The trouble was that unlike my Boss I was full to bursting. I thought that maybe I could manage a spot of cheese. To the chief steward I said: 'I'll just have a piece of Stilton and a glass of red wine.'

'Would you care to choose the wine, sir?' he invited me.

More magic words! The wine was stored under the stairwell. I rummaged around the rack, and settled for a bottle with a distinctive label: *Chateau Lafitte Rothschild 1959.*

Yes, that would do nicely.

I sipped my glass, and found the contents – well, rather special. That is to say, out of this world. Later I would tell friends it was like 'angels dancing on my tongue'. I helped myself to another.

There was no sign of the Cap'n, so I went ahead on my own, demolishing one, two, three glasses while ploughing into the Stilton.

That was when Simon Grigg who was by now a good friend of mine appeared from the galley. He saw the bottle, and his complexion changed.

'Dear me,' he said, or a four-letter word to that effect. 'Who on earth has opened that bottle?'

'I did,' I said. 'Why? Does it matter?'

'*Matter*!' he exploded. 'Do you know what you're drinking? That bottle is – was – a personal gift to the Chairman from President Mitterand for Mr Maxwell's birthday tomorrow. It costs £750 a bottle!'

'Strewth!' I thought. 'Now I really am for it.' Suddenly the day didn't look as rosy as it had looked half an hour ago, and neither did my future.

There was only one thing for it: to go and face the music. With Robert Maxwell, as I mentioned, I had learned that when you were in trouble, always hold your hands up in surrender. Above all, tell the truth. And I was in big trouble.

I made my way to the stern, and knocked on the door of the Satellite Room where I knew Bob would be on the phone to London.

I couldn't have timed a worse moment.

The Cap'n was in a foul mood. I could tell the minute I walked in – mainly by the way he slammed the phone back into its cradle as if he was trying to break it. Whatever he had heard, he didn't like.

'What do you want?' he bellowed. All traces of his earlier affability had vanished.

Jesus! I thought. How do I tell him?

'I've got a confession to make to you, R.M.,' I blurted out.

'What – ?'

'I've just drunk half your birthday present from the French President!'

There was a pause. Then an odd smile spread over his face. 'What was it?'

I told him. *'Chateau Lafitte Rothschild 1959.'*

He surveyed me for a long moment. 'You have very good taste, Mister. Now fuck off and leave me alone. I'm busy.' And he turned back to his desk.

Sometimes, I thought, I'm never going to understand this man.

I went back to the saloon and finished off the bottle. Well, it seemed a shame to waste it.

CHAPTER SEVEN

Mission to Moscow

18 October 1990. Appropriately, we are ensconced in the Octobre Hotel, Moscow. The Maxwell entourage includes the Deputy Chairman of MCC, Jean-Pierre Anselmini, Chief of Staff Peter Jay, and myself.

The Chairman had led the delegation with a view to 'proudly presenting' the second volume of the speeches and writings of General Secretary Mikhail Sergeevich Gorbachev to the Russian President in person, and later immortalising said scriptures in print around the world.

But first, as we await word for an audience in the Kremlin, a few hiccups. We have had a difficult day. A lot of meetings, to no obvious avail. The Chairman is getting impatient, kicking his heels at the delay. Bob never did like being kept waiting.

Around four p.m. I found myself sitting in the presidential suite of the hotel, watching the Boss polish off yet another jar of caviar (at a modest ten dollars a tub) washed down with the inevitable chilled Stolichnaya, his favourite vodka that he always required chilled in the deep freeze because its specific gravity doesn't allow it to become frozen.

In rushes Jean-Pierre. In his thick French accent, he announces: 'There are four very important rabbits to meet you downstairs, Chairman!'

Even the boss looks taken aback at that one.

'What the fuck do I want to see a bunch of rabbits for?'

'Bob, you must see them. They are very important.'

The Chairman turns to me, and shrugs with that look of his that betokens mischief in the air.

'Send the fucking rabbits up.'

They duly arrive, four of them garbed in orthodox Jewish robes, complete with wide-brimmed black hats like a quartet of Fagins from *Oliver Twist*.

They stare at us, wondering why the reception committee is doubled up.

'Oh – ' Bob controlled himself with an effort.

'Do come in, gentlemen! What can I do for you?'

To this day, I still don't know what they were there for. Presumably they were holding out the begging bowl for some cause. Bob heard them out, shook their hands, watched them leave. And once the door was closed, held his ample sides with laughter. As an unorthodox Jew, he could see the funny side. From then on, Rabbis would always be rabbits.

Ten minutes later, the call came. Tea and cakes in the Kremlin with the President of all the Russias.

Big time. Probably the most impressive meeting in all the corridors of power I was ever privileged to tread with Cap'n Bob.

The Boss had even arranged for a special edition of the speeches, bound in leather, that he himself would present to the General Secretary. Mr Snapper would be recording the event for posterity – and, no doubt, for the front page of the *Daily Mirror*.

This was part of the series on world figures that Pergamon Press had been rolling out over the months under the umbrella title *Pergamon Leaders of the World*. Others had included Poland's General Jaruzelski, and the Chinese leader Deng Xiaoping.

I had, in fact, been given an early glimpse in the Chairman's office of this last tome, which proudly announced that Deng was 'Chairman of the Advisory Commission of the Chinese Communist Party's Central Committee' . . . at which point I drew a deep breath . . . 'considered the driving force behind China's programme of economic and social reform, and principal architect of his country's open policy to the outside world.' At which point my eyes glazed over.

One reviewer of this sure-fire hit series unkindly pointed out: 'These collections of the wit and wisdom of sundry leaders traditionally conclude with an interview with Robert Maxwell.'

But, best-sellers or not, it was our ticket to ride into the Kremlin. Through the front door.

The letter which had started the ball rolling came from Peter Jay, Chief of Staff, to His Excellency Leonaid Zamyatin, Ambassador of the USSR in Kensington.

It emphasised: 'We therefore seek your good offices . . . in arranging a suitable occasion during Mr Maxwell's visit to Moscow for him personally to present this volume . . .' etc, etc . . .

But it was the key that unlocked the door to one of the most secret inner sanctums in the world.

In the suite, the phone rang. A car was waiting downstairs.

'Wait here,' Bob ordered Peter Jay.'And answer the phone!' He could be quite brusque at times.

The black government Sherka whisked the pair of us down the middle of the three-lane highway – strictly reserved for VIPs, visiting dignitaries, KGB officers and assorted spies. Beside the driver sat a pallid-faced official in a long black overcoat from the Interior Office who had been designated to escort us.

Beyond the blacked-out windows, traffic clogged the rest of the road in an endless jam. On the pavements, I watched crowds of grey-faced Muscovites struggling back from work in the early evening rush hour.

We drove smoothly on at 70 miles per hour, without braking once. At each junction, uniformed police held up the traffic and waved us through with their batons.

One law for the rich, one for the poor. Even in the seat of Communism.

'This is what power is all about, Mike,' said Cap'n Bob. Even he was impressed. 'Didn't I promise you this would happen to you one day?'

If he had, I'd forgotten it.

Keeping in step outside the Kremlin.

'Yes, R.M.,' I said.

But first, a detour to take in Lenin's tomb. The obligatory visit for any official guest.

The usual queue was huddled along one whole length of Red Square to pay its respects to the Bolshevik revolutionary, still lying in state 66 years after his death from a stroke in 1924. Clusters of school children. Groups of elderly Party workers bussed in from miles around, whether they wanted to or not. No excuses for not turning up, Comrade.

A chill autumn wind was blowing the first hint of winter across the cobbled square, all the way from Siberia. We pulled our coat collars up, and followed our official guide to the entrance. He had a murmured word with the uniformed guard on duty.

The khaki-clad soldier raised an imperious hand to the shuffling throng, and they came to a halt. An officer appeared from nowhere. More muttered words.

'This way,' said our guide.

The officer turned his back on us, and began marking time. Bob looked at me, and shrugged. Into marching order. The Cap'n followed suit, his huge bulk lifting and falling behind the officer.

Up, down. Up, down.

I did the same, marching on the spot, our feet ringing on the stones. This would not be the last time I found myself struggling to keep step with Cap'n Bob.

Then, at a signal, we were off. Just the three of us, the officer leading. The ex-soldier came out in the Chairman, and he responded with relish.

Slow march. Funereal pace.

Well, we were in a sepulchre, after all.

Along a stone passage, through a door, up some steps, alongside a railing – and then we were looking down on the old rogue himself.

The bald-headed alabaster face stared unseeingly up at the vaulted ceiling, just as it had done for six decades. A guide reminded us how Lenin had been born Vladimir Ilyich Ulyanov in 1870, how he had been exiled to Siberia in 1895 for subversive activities, and how he went abroad to study Marx's theories. And finally how the German government secretly helped him travel to Petrograd from Switzerland to mastermind the uprising against Kerensky's rule in 1917. 'On 25 October, Lenin led the Bolshevik overthrow,' the guide intoned.

'That's the Russian calendar. By our date, it was 7 November,' said the Chairman knowledgeably.

I was impressed. It's amazing what you can learn in four minutes.

Amazing, too, that a month later I should read in London that one of Lenin's ears actually dropped off in full view of the latter-day mourners.

'At least it was only his ear,' said Cap'n Bob, when I showed him the cutting.

You don't actually stand to admire the ghostly-pale face of one of history's more famous revolutionaries. You keep moving at a slow but steady pace on the high stone walkway around and above it – until you are in another passage and suddenly spirited out into the open air again.

It is actually quite shivery to know that you are about to be the personal guest of one of the two most important men in the world. The other, at that time, being Ronald Reagan, who was also a pal of Cap'n Bob.

In Red Square. (Picture by Robert Maxwell)

On that grey October day I thought we were going to be a cosy threesome. Two Chairmen, and me. Wrong. A fourth figure turned up for the party. Vladimir Kruschkov. In case it has slipped your memory – or if you never knew – friend Vlad was Chairman of the KGB, no less.

Three Chairmen, one Lincoln Imp.

Let me tell you about the Lincoln Imp. I had it concealed in my pocket, the famous emblem of my home town, a gold-plated Imp which is the hallmark of Lincoln and used by all and sundry, especially the Tourist Office, to promote the city. If the chance came, I wanted to give my imp to President Gorbachev.

The Sherka slid round the great walls of the Kremlin, and stopped outside the private entrance. We were saluted through the heavy doors, and into a labyrinth of corridors until we reached into the heart of the Kremlin, an inner sanctum seldom seen by outsiders below the status of world leader.

Large men with small eyes in blue lounge suits with padded shoulders, the kind we used to see in tailors' windows in the '50s, ushered us through. The only difference being that part of the padding in their jackets belonged to pistols concealed in holsters under their armpits. Kremlin issue.

A lift took us up four floors to Gorbachev's private quarters overlooking Red Square and the dismal queues waiting in the gathering dusk like the night before a Christmas sale.

And the world changed.

It's the little things that count, I always say. After the third-rate quality of everything we had seen outside, the kind that the patient Russian people endured in their GUM superstores and tawdry shop fronts, Aladdin's Cave opened before our eyes.

'This way, gentlemen.' Gorby's private secretary had met us at the lift.

The room was large and spacious. The centrepiece was a long table on which you could have played snooker, covered in green velvet, seating twelve people on either side. The Kremlin Crucible. On the side, the finest bone china. Portraits and oil paintings around the walls.

Gorby greeted the Cap'n like an old friend. An embrace, typical Russian, but no kiss. I couldn't help noticing that his small hands couldn't meet behind Maxwell's massive 22-stone back if they'd tried.

As the President spoke, an interpreter went through the verbal motions.

'Mr Maxwell, a pleasure to see you again.'

'Secretary General – ' Bob knew when to be formal – 'the pleasure is all mine.' He crushed the smaller man to his massive chest.

The Boss turned to me. 'Can I introduce you to – '

'We have met already. Hello, Mike!'

I was reminded of the fact that Robert Maxwell spoke nine languages, but understood 12.

My only Russian was da (yes), niet (no), pivo (beer), and 'gde tualet?' ('Can you direct me to the toilet?') which I figured were enough to get me by when it came down to basics.

Gorbachev gestured at his large desk by the window. And there, laid out on the desk, were six large ten-by-eight colour prints of his last meeting with the Boss which I had taken at the memorable lunch in Minnesota, plus a shot with his wife Raisa – for which he had already ordered 50 copies.

Good God, I thought. The man is not only a diplomat – he has a heart, too. No wonder Margaret Thatcher called him 'a great Westerner'.

Bob outside the KGB headquarters.

We sat down. He introduced the fourth man, the KGB chief. A silent Suit poured tea – the finest Earl Grey, with cakes on a silver platter. I fired off some shots of the pair of them together.

Twenty minutes of chat ensued. All the time my mind was working. *What's the picture going to be?* Because this is the picture the Old Man will want for his album, for posterity, and for the *Mirror*.

I managed a shot of my Chairman handing over the bound leather book to its appreciative recipient.

Suddenly, in the middle of the affability and without warning, a phone buzzed on the desk. One of nine multi-coloured telephones – most of them grey, several black, one red.

The red phone.

Christ, the hot line!

Gorbachev threw a swift signal at the Suits. They left the room in a hurry, like a small rugger scrum chasing a loose ball, taking Bob and myself with them. Along with the Chairman of the KGB.

All at once we were on the outside, looking in.

I saw my picture vanishing without trace, before it had even been taken. I'd lost it! I would never see him again.

Later I would learn that indeed it had been Ronald Reagan on the phone, calling from the White House.

Outside, in the passage, we stood like lost souls. 'R.M.,' I said. 'I'm really upset. Do you realise what I've just missed?'

'What do you mean, Mister?'

'I had this great picture in mind – of you with the two most powerful men in this whole nation. And we've missed it.'

Cap'n Bob saw it too, and his shoulders shrugged ruefully in acceptance of the fickle finger of fate. It was a typical Maxwell gesture of the inevitable.

Fifteen minutes passed. Fifteen very long minutes. Bob kept talking to the KGB Chairman, in Russian.

Then, suddenly, the door opened. Gorbachev emerged, clutching an armful of papers. I had my Leica poised round my neck, and acted without thinking.

As Mikhail appeared, I don't know what possessed me – but I grabbed him by the arm.

'Mr President,' I implored, 'I just need one more photograph.' All right, I had two of them together, Gorby and Bob, but not the three.

Yak, yak, yak went the interpreter.

I walked him a few paces to Cap'n Bob and Vladimir.

That's when I saw Bob's mouth drop in stupefaction. Was his personal photographer really manhandling the President of the USSR?

Tense moments: with President Gorbachev and KGB chief, Vladimir Kruschkov. Behind me, the security guards are going for their guns . . .

. . . but then, it's all smiles.

Indeed he was.

I lined them up, the three of them like a firing squad against the wall, and shot off five frames in rapid succession on the motor drive.

Click-click-click!

What I hadn't seen was the pantomime going on behind me, as the Blue Suits reached inside their breast pockets as one man for their pistols – and drew them.

Oblivious to the panic in the corridor, I took my pictures with the gun-toting KGB men waving their guns behind me.

'Thank you, Mr President.'

That was when I reached in my pocket and brought out my Lincoln Imp. 'May I also present you with this memento from the City of Lincoln!'

The President took it, examined it closely, then nodded and fixed the tiny gold medallion in his lapel. He seemed amused, but preoccupied.

'Thank you, Mike.'

My thoughts went back to that phone call. I just hoped no one had done anything silly in a missile silo.

Afterwards, back in the limousine, Cap'n Bob turned to me. 'Do you realise what you just did?' he said sternly. 'You could have got us both shot!'

Then: 'But I have to say I have never seen anyone operate like that in my life.' And a big grin spread over his face.

In the seven years I worked personally for Robert Maxwell, I found myself in Russia a number of times. The Boss was doing a lot of business with the Ruskies, and seemed to think I was useful in some way if only to be on call with my camera. For myself, I was always looking out for a good picture.

I also got to know the dreaded Lubyanka rather well. The place where, as the saying went, a lot of people went in, but not an awful lot of people came out.

The KGB headquarters on Dzerzhinsky Square is a gloomy looking building, deceptively featureless, and from the outside could pass for just another third-rate hotel. Bleak and blank – except for a certain noticeable security on the doors.

I was treated to a number of meals in the second floor dining-room with the top brass of the KGB, some of whose names I knew, most that I didn't.

This time it was a private room along the passage, and dinner for ten. Starting early, at seven p.m. I was at one end of the candle-lit table, with the Boss in pride of place two seats away so that he could command the attention of everybody.

Our host was Vladimir Kruschkov, aforesaid head of the KGB, seated

Inside the corridors of power at the Kremlin. (Picture by Robert Maxwell)

opposite Bob. The occasion: to mark a new chapter in the Chairman's relations with the Soviet hierarchy. A new tome of speeches or witticisms that would go a bundle in Mother Russia but, I suspected, not figure too highly among the 75,000 titles published annually across the board in the U.K.

After the initial obligatory toasts of neat vodka, all of us standing erect and formal behind our chairs, we sat down to a gourmet's feast of fish, fowl and venison that would have found its place into any Michelin Guide. The wines were hearty French.

For myself, I felt the usual mix of excitement and unease at being in this strangest and most unnerving of dining halls. Knowing full well that two floors up were the cells where unspeakable things were rumoured to have happened to 'enemies of the State'.

Up until then, I suppose like most civilians, I had imagined that the cells were in the basement, out of reach and out of earshot. But I was wrong – they were on the fourth floor. How do I know? Because after the fifth vodka toast I asked the man on my right, and he told me.

The man on my right was Mr Valery Baldin, a slim, thinning-haired individual aged about 50, in a smart grey suit – who happened to be the

Deputy Premier, one notch in the pecking order below Gorbachev himself. He was a friendly, lively sort, and we had conversed animatedly in pidgin English, a lot of sign language, and with the help of an interpreter sitting on a chair behind us when the going got hard.

But the conversation flowed – and so did the Stolichnaya.

If you have never been hosted by a Russian, you cannot possibly understand the rhythm and the ritual of the toasting that is a basic tradition of any meal. Which is why the proceedings get more boisterous as the evening wears on – even in the Lubyanka, where jollity is not normally a by-word. On that night it seemed to me that every other sentence led into a toast.

The Boss understood it, even if I didn't. I would listen to a gibberish of Russian, and when it came to the name 'Mr Maxwell!' – everyone rose to their feet and drained their glass of vodka, which was immediately replenished by waiters in white jackets from behind.

I became quite adept at spotting the word 'Maxwell' and rising to my feet on cue. We were up and down like yo-yos.

Towards the end of the feast, there was an interruption. The door opened, and a man came in and walked straight up to Krushkov, bent and whispered in his ear. The KGB chief frowned, then nodded. He leaned over and said something to Bob, whose eyebrows rose almost to his hairline.

It was an expression I had come to know that meant not just surprise, but pleasurable surprise.

Sure enough, he looked down the table at me, his big face aglow. 'The First Secretary wants to meet me – now!'

That meant the Boss wanted me there, too. But as we both rose, he added: 'I'm sorry, Mike. I can't get you in to the Kremlin this time. They've only sanctioned one car.'

I was still not altogether clear what was going on, or about this sudden shift in our schedule. But I knew one thing, and voiced it loudly and formally. I didn't want to be left in the Lubyanka, but I did want to get back inside the Kremlin and not miss another major photo opportunity.

'Mr Maxwell,' I declared. 'I need to be there with you. I'll travel in the boot!'

The Boss shook his head with a rueful smile. 'It's a nice idea, Mike. But I don't think so.'

An official Cherka was waiting downstairs, with the hammer-and-sickle fluttering from the bonnet and an impassive driver at the wheel. There was room for three passengers – Maxwell up front with the driver, the KGB chief and Baldin in the back.

I stood beside them as guards sprang to open doors. Then I took the bull by the horns – or the bear by the muzzle – and said: 'Excuse me, Mr Baldin, but do you think I could sit on your lap?'

The interpreter translated. There was the briefest of silences – then the Russian threw back his head in an uproarious laugh.

'*Da!*' he said. '*Da!*'

What a great sense of humour that man had.

And that was how we went through the dark streets of Moscow from the KGB headquarters to the Kremlin, with Mr Snapper squashing the Deputy Premier of the USSR into the cushions at the back with one arm round his neck.

Bob turned in his seat to look back at us, and just shook his head slowly in disbelief.

Afterwards, with a half-hour meeting in the President's private office under his belt and a roll of film safely in my pocket to record it, my Chairman and I were driven back to our hotel.

Cap'n Bob turned to me. 'Mister, do you know what you were doing? Do you know whose lap you were sitting on? I'll be dining out on this for weeks.'

'So will I, R.M.,' I said. 'So will I.'

CHAPTER EIGHT

Rich and Running

The weekend of 10 June 1988 should be ringed in gold, then framed, and hung on my study wall in memory of the greatest extravaganza that even the extravagant Robert Maxwell ever put on.

The occasion: Cap'n Bob's 65th birthday party at H.H.H. – otherwise Headington Hill Hall, his stately pile on the outskirts of Oxford. You'll find it down a hill on the right behind a high wall as you drive in to the city from the London Road.

'It's a major milestone, Mike,' he had boomed at me in his office earlier in the week. 'You're not 65 every day. I don't want any mistakes.'

'No, Publisher. There won't be any,' I assured him.

I had been called in to discuss the photographic arrangements for recording this major milestone for posterity. A thought occurred to me: 'Now you can claim your bus pass, R.M.!' I said. To which jollity, thank heaven, he gave a short laugh.

The birthday would be an occasion for much celebration, tributes to Maxwellomania, and utter exhaustion.

By happy chance, the date coincided with the 40th anniversary of Maxwell's pet company, Pergamon Press, so a lot of the outlay could be written off against tax.

Cap'n Bob handed me a sheet of paper across the desk. When I looked at it, my jaw dropped a few notches.

The festivities would go on all weekend. Starting on Friday (his actual birthday), and concluding with a seminar on Monday for the firm's middle-management employees. They would doubtless have preferred to be back at their desks nursing a hangover rather than dreaming up bright ideas to improve on Pergamon's profits. But after the feast comes the reckoning.

I glanced through the schedule, assessing photo opportunities. I would have six photographers under me, and my instructions were simple. *Don't miss a trick!*

If anything went wrong – and I would have broken out in a cold sweat if I started thinking what *could* go wrong – it was my neck on the line. I would have to do the decent thing, and fall on my tripod.

The guest list had been prepared by his social staff, and read like a page torn from *Who's Who?*.

Make that several pages.

On the manicured lawns outside the imposing front doors of Chateau Maxwell, four large marquees would be erected – large enough to hold 1,400 people. They would find three-foot-square portraits of the Boss beaming out at them from each marquee, in case anyone was unsure who the birthday boy was.

Friday night kicked off with an eight-course dinner for 500 VIP guests, white tie required, seated at tables of eight.

Saturday's festivities began with a lunch-time buffet for 1,400 people (standing up, but with a few chairs and tables scattered around the tent for the elderly and infirm).

Saturday night was an elegant black-tie dinner for 700, at tables of ten. I shook my head, trying to figure out the guest list.

'Who *are* all these people?'

'Bob's personal friends,' voiced one of the organisers.

Who was it who said sarcasm is the lowest form of wit?

On Sunday, the shindig would approach its final stages with another lunchtime buffet for 1,400, ending with a presentation from Cap'n Bob to loyal long-service employees.

The cabaret matched the occasion. On Bob's actual birthday night, no less than the National Ballet Company had been hired to entertain him. Bob actually didn't like ballet very much, but the name did carry a certain prestige and it looked good on the invitations.

On Saturday night, the entire cast from *42nd Street* would sing numbers from the hit West End show which had just ended its run. Impresario Harvey Goldsmith had put everything together, at a reported fee of £85,000.

Working it out later, I figured the whole shenanigans had set Bob back close to half a million pounds. Speaking personally, it was the most extravagant birthday party I had ever witnessed or could hope to see again.

As C-in-C of the photo 'shoot' I dutifully gathered my team, issuing instructions like a military operation.

Photographers with 35mm and polaroid cameras, colour film, to report to me at 7 p.m. They will be dressed in dinner jackets. Photographers will take shots at random

Me and my team at the celebrations.

before dinner, particularly of people being greeted by the Chairman. As soon as the guests sit down to dinner, the photographers will start taking pictures of couples at each table. They will shoot the table number, followed by the couples.

'A trifle extreme,' I said to Jean Baddeley, who was masterminding the operation. 'We don't want blood on the lawn.'

As soon as they have finished each film, it will be handed to a runner who will get it to the motor-bike messenger waiting to take it to the studio. The courier will return to H.H.H. immediately after delivering the first rolls, to collect the next batch of films.

As the studio completes the photographs, they will be placed into presentation folders, together with a suitable Pergamon message, and put into plastic bags per table, with a sheet in each bag denoting the table number. The bags will then be transported back to H.H.H. and delivered to the appropriate table for the guests.

And all that before the coffee starts to get cold!

Looking back, I have never seen so many people walking on so many eggs over so many days, waiting for something to go wrong. But in the end, amazingly, it didn't.

The big night was Friday. Bob, resplendent in white tie and tails, strode around like Napoleon encouraging his troops before Waterloo. Finally he stood on the stone steps leading to the terrace with more than a dozen of his family clustered around him, while a military band in full dress uniform marched past like the Changing of the Guard.

The last number that some bright soul had thought up, as the band paced

March past at Bob's 65th birthday.

solemnly across the lawn and out of sight round the corner of the house, was the old Beatles hit *Maxwell's Silver Hammer*.

Bob was probably the only one present who didn't know it. He turned to me as the strains faded away and applause filled the warm night air.

'What was that song, Mike?'

'I'm not sure, R.M.' I had enough champagne inside me to risk pulling his leg. 'It could have been Colonel Bogey . . .'

'Ah, yes.'

And ah, yes, a night to remember.

One postscript to the party came a week later, in the form of a letter sent to him by Hugh Cudlipp, a former *Daily Mirror* editor and a legendary name in

Fleet Street. As an elder statesman in the game, and someone who had the ear of just about everybody, he had been hired as a consultant – and was one of the few people I knew who didn't care what he said to the Old Man.

Thus it was that a letter that landed on Bob's desk suggesting he staunch the flow in the paper of his own name. 'By now every man, woman and child in the land must be aware that you are the *Mirror*'s proprietor,' Cudlipp wrote. Possibly this was because on Monday, Maxwell's name was mentioned 74 times, on Tuesday 63 times and on Wednesday 94 times. 'This must surely earn a place in the *Guinness Book of Records*,' Cudlipp added caustically.

I cannot say the Boss appeared to notice, but the flow did slacken after that. And this was the man who the year before had told a shareholders' meeting: 'I don't go in for ego trips. It's not my style . . . '

The first time I actually set foot inside the magnificent stately home had been at the behest of Betty Maxwell to commemorate an earlier birthday. She gathered the entire family there one weekend for a special birthday portrait to record the great dynasty for posterity.

Over the years, Betty Maxwell would become a friend who welcomed me into her circle with a genuine warmth that made me feel part of this extraordinary family. She herself had been the daughter of prosperous French parents – her father Paul was a cavalry officer who enjoyed a marvellously chequered lifestyle which, as she once told me in her lilting French accent, had earned him the nickname of *Chic, Cheque and Shock!* Why, *père* Paul was even alleged to have danced with Mata Hari.

History has chronicled her turbulent marriage to the charismatic young captain who won her heart during the war years. The fact that their marriage would last almost half a century speaks volumes for Betty's capacity to be there when Bob needed her, and quietly to go her own route as the matriarch of the family while Bob was making massive headlines as the showman of his own destiny – which is why she was instrumental in calling the whole family together that day.

I took extra care in packing my camera case. In fact I took a complete mobile studio: tripod, lamps, a stock of lenses, the lot. I couldn't afford any mistakes, as the Maxwell progeny were travelling in from far and wide.

I drove down the M40 to Oxford, and turned down the London Road towards the old town. The Chairman had been in residence for a quarter of a century, but it was Betty who really loved the place.

Headington had, in fact, originally been hired out as headquarters for Bob's expanding Pergamon Press, and rented off the local council for the incredibly small sum of £2,000 a year. Then, in 1971 after a lot of high-level boardroom manoeuvring, Bob persuaded Pergamon to grant him a lease until 1999 for an annual rent of £1,100 'exclusive of overheads'.

The previous tenants before 1960 had been the Red Cross, who had built

H.H.H. outside view, plus helicopter.

four bungalow-style office buildings in the grounds, which proved ideal for the staff. The Cap'n would refer jocularly to his estate as 'my council house', secure in the knowledge that it was the best bargain in the country.

Up a winding drive, and there it was – a three-storey colonnaded mansion built from local sandstone, rising like a French chateau out of manicured green lawns and hedgerows into the summer sunshine. There are some sights you don't forget in life, and this was one of them.

Over the years, as I got to know H.H.H. like a second home, I would never lose that jolt of pleasure when I came off the busy London Road into an oasis of calm and quietness.

Well, perhaps quietness wasn't exactly the order of that first day. Not when you've got five strident grandchildren and two toddlers racing around, creating merry hell on the polished wooden floor.

In all, there were 17 of the Maxwell brood collected that day – either direct descendants or related by marriage. I thought of posing them on the stone

Family Portrait. Only Cap'n Bob was missing.

steps outside the house that led up from the main lawn, but the balustrades needed a good sanding down and I decided against it.

Instead I opted for the splendid staircase in the Great Hall, set under cream arches and framed by two gleaming white pillars. I spent half an hour setting up my 'studio', and then came the task of summoning them all together.

'Right, if you sit here . . . and there . . . and put that little girl on your knee please, madam . . . ' I knew Ian and Kevin, and of course Betty, but I had no idea who the rest were.

Finally, all was ready. Then I looked around.

Someone was missing.

Someone rather important.

'Er – has anyone seen the Chairman?' I asked.

'He's here somewhere,' a voice said. 'I think . . .'

But they were wrong. Cap'n Bob was back in London. He had either forgotten all about it, or simply couldn't be bothered to make the trek.

I took the pictures anyway. And afterwards, when I showed them to her, a philosophical Mrs Maxwell said: 'Ah well, perhaps we can superimpose Bob's head in at the back!'

But we never got round to it, and my portrait of the Maxwell dynasty remains without its founder to this day.

Now at last I can own up to a guilty secret.

Often I stayed overnight at Headington. Sometimes with Cap'n Bob around, other times with Betty and the family. I was allowed the run of the

Kevin and Ian.

Headington Hill Hall wine cellar

place and treated like any house guest, enjoying the most sumptuous meals washed down with the finest wines.

One of my favourite areas to explore was indeed the wine cellar. There must have been 10,000 bottles down there in the basement that ran beneath most of the mansion. Among them was a collection of 'blue-chip' vintages – the kind that mature into a small fortune.

Top of the list were the 1945, 1949 and 1953 clarets, with later vintages of 1988 and 1989 on other shelves. Cap'n Bob enjoyed vintage port, particularly in the days when he was smoking his favourite *Cohiba* cigars, and I spotted the legendary 1947 and 1955 years tucked away on the lower shelves cocooned in their reassuring film of dust.

My personal disaster happened after Bob called me up to his office one day, and said: 'I want you to photograph Headington Hill Hall, Mike. Every room. Take as long as you need over it. And don't forget the wine cellar!'

'I won't, R.M.'

As if I could.

But before I reached my personal Mecca of the cellars, I performed my duties above ground. Prowling the 14 acres of the estate to capture stables and swimming pool, tennis court and hidden arbours. Away from the rat race, the atmosphere was as peaceful as a monastery.

Inside the Hall there were 13 bedrooms, most of them with *en suite* bathrooms. My own, complete with four-poster bed, faced west and looked out through picture windows to Oxford's dreaming spires and majestic domes.

The place dated back to 1851, when it had been built by a local brewer named James Morrell. In 1946 after World War II it was commandeered by the Government and converted into a hospital.

Maxwell's own double bed was a massive king-size affair measuring six-foot-seven, reinforced and with a padded headboard. Outside, in a passage leading to it, was a cartoon showing (if anyone had doubted it) that he did have a sense of humour after all. It was a portrait all in red of R.M. himself – as the Devil, complete with small horns sprouting from his head and clutching a three-pronged fork.

'What do you think of it, Mike?' he asked me once.

To which I did *not* reply: 'A perfect likeness, Chairman!'

Actually, it was close.

Back to the wine cellar. In the bowels of the Hall I snapped away down the serried ranks of cases. Impressive, but, after a time, a little 'samey'.

So I thought up something different.

I found a dozen bottles of *Chateau Romanee-Conti 1978*, an impressive looking Burgundy, nestling alongside the *'82 Mouton-Rothschild*. And next to them, three dusty bottles of *Chateau Montrose '45*.

Beautiful!

I took out four bottles of the *Romanee-Conti*, and put them at the end of one of the rows. Then, ever so carefully, placed three bottles of the *Mouton-Rothschild* on top, followed by two of the *Montrose*. The third *Montrose* went on the peak to complete the pyramid.

Now *that* would impress the Old Man.

But as I turned away, the top bottle wobbled – and toppled. The whole lot started to go over as I dived to get my arms under them before they hit the stone floor. And I succeeded – apart from one.

Crash!

What else but the *Montrose*?

(above) My four poster bed at H.H.H.   *(below) Elegant lounge, H.H.H.*

(above) Bob's bed at H.H.H.   *(below) Great Hall, H.H.H.*

(above) TV room at H.H.H.

(below) Dining-room, H.H.H.

Much later, after I had discreetly cleared up the broken glass and swabbed away the precious red liquid, scrubbing the stains off the floor, I found out the cost. Just a casual enquiry.

How much is a bottle of Montrose '45?

Pergamon had paid £1,100 for the three. Which meant just over £365 pounds down the drain.

I never did own up, and no one ever noticed. But now I'm confessing.

Sorry, R.M.

Robert Maxwell was rich and running, and I was happy to keep pace with him. By now he had been listed as Britain's eighth wealthiest man, and he continued to show every intention of living up to it.

Admittedly a lot of my work for him as his personal photographer was after hours, in my own time, and played havoc with my social life. But for the sheer excitement and adrenalin buzz, it was worth every minute.

The ritual was invariably the same. A call from the Ninth Floor. 'The Old Man wants to see you. Now!'

And from behind his desk, the Boss: 'Right, Mike. We're going to (such-and-such a place). Tomorrow.' It could be San Francisco, the West Indies, Budapest, New York, Tokyo, Prague – anywhere. Once it was even China, and somehow there was a visa in my passport.

The Maxwell machine was unstoppable.

His wealth, his fame – or notoriety, depending on which side of the fence you stood – and his lifestyle made him an instant target for ribaldry, reluctant respect and ridicule. And jokes.

Like the famous *Knock! Knock!* gag that went round the *Mirror*.

Who's there?

Bob –

Bob who?

You're fired!

Cartoonists had a field day. In fact, Bob didn't really mind. He only banged off shoals of those equally notorious legal writs if he felt his business dealings had been slighted.

And he just loved to see his face in the paper, even if it came from a pen instead of a camera. In January 1985, for instance, he was awarded the Gold Joker Trophy by the Cartoonists Club of Great Britain for being 'our greatest source of inspiration over the past year'.

I went with him to the Cartoonist pub in Shoe Lane, located below the old Press Club premises. At the ceremony, surrounded by some of the Street's funniest and wittiest figures, he was asked how important a sense

Cartoon time.

of humour was in his business.

'If you don't have one, I feel sorry for you,' Bob retorted immediately, as he accepted a souvenir pin to mark the occasion. Looking at it, he added: 'I will wear this on the seat of my trousers so that when I get too pompous it will prick me hard!'

As we all raised our glasses with a suitable cheer, I overheard one cartoonist mutter darkly to another: 'His backside's going to look like a pin cushion inside a month.'

Once, though, a cartoon did overstep the mark – though without the creator's knowledge or consent. I heard about it when I dropped by the Ninth Floor to check the schedule for the week.

'The Old Man's in a foul mood.' An air of doom and gloom hung low over the outer office, as it always did when Bob was upset. Like ripples in a lake, the mark of his temper would emanate out through that door marked PRIVATE and affect the outer office and eventually the entire building. If the Publisher was in a bad temper, and showed up on the Editorial floor, strong men would quake and keep their heads below the battlements.

I know. I've seen it.

'What is it this time?' I asked Debbie Dines at her desk by the window. 'What's happened?'

With the typical raunchy humour you tend to find in Oz, she was trying not to laugh. 'It's the Griffin cartoon in the paper today. Someone's doctored it!'

And indeed, someone had. It was a drawing of the Berlin Wall, the backdrop for the latest effort from our marvellous satirical cartoonist. Except that someone had written on it two rather unkind words. *Fuck Maxwell*.

Which didn't exactly go down a treat with the Publisher, especially when the rival *Sun* spotted it and duly had a field day at Bob's expense.

Charles Griffin, of course, denied it was by his own pen. Rightly protesting that 'When I draw a cartoon it goes through a lot of hands before it gets in the paper. I am completely innocent.' An inquiry was launched, with predictable results. Nothing.

Other organs were equally uncharitable. *Private Eye* dubbed him MacSwell as Bob's girth burgeoned, and of course produced the long-running strip cartoon charting the Cap'n's uneven course through the shark-infested financial waters around him.

Another incident had all of us in the outer office in hysterics – though our laughter never penetrated to Maxwell's ear. The Nine O'Clock News on BBC TV led with an item about a top West German spy who had defected to Russia with vital NATO secrets. They had no suitable photograph to illustrate the story, but came up with the imaginative wheeze of showing a large sinister figure in silhouette to represent the spy.

Guess who they picked? No one in the BBC News Department recognised the bulky outline – but Bob did. He was not amused. He elicited a fulsome apology from the top brass.

Citizen Bob saw himself as a newspaper baron built in the Northcliffe mould, and had taken to his role with gusto. 'Did you know, Mike,' he confided one evening, as the two of us raised a glass of bubbly together in his office. 'That man once promoted a lift boy to Foreign Editor on the spot. And it worked!'

I thought he might be leading up to something, and sensed immediate promotion. In vain. I should have known better, of course. Bob was just musing about life as he tended to do from time to time. All you were expected to do was sit and listen, with the occasional appreciative nod.

In fact I found myself enjoying those sessions more and more after work, when I had dropped into the Chairman's office to show him a batch of photos – and been invited to stay while the champagne corks popped.

Did we have fun? Well, life was exciting, and totally unpredictable. Rumours abounded in those heady days. Like the one that our Chairman was planning to install a loudspeaker system in all three newsrooms (*Daily Mirror, Sunday Mirror, The People*) so that he could broadcast daily exhortations to the staff without leaving his desk.

Shades of Big Brother. Sadly, it never happened.

To be fair, the Cap'n could take a joke against himself, though he usually insisted on coming up with the last word.

And, for anyone who dared, you never knew how he would take it, or which way he would jump.

But one evening in his study on the Tenth Floor at Maxwell House I found him chortling over a story that had appeared in a local paper in the West Country. Half a dozen others in the room were laughing, too, and it seemed the mirth was genuine rather than sycophantic.

I raised an eyebrow. Bob spotted me, and beckoned me over. 'Come and see this, Mike!'.

A copy of the *Western Morning News* was spread out on his desk. I peered over his shoulder.

The report was about a bright green budgerigar named Buster that had disappeared from its cage in the village of Paulton, near Bath. Buster could be identified by the only words he knew – a squawk of 'Bloody Maxwell! Bloody Maxwell!'.

It seemed the bird was owned by a worker who had been made redundant in one of Maxwell's companies, and the budgie had apparently picked up its master's views on his late boss.

'I hope they find it,' said the Chairman. 'But I just wish that bird was broadcasting a different message.'

On a more serious note – and Bob basically thought of himself as very serious, with none of the pricks from his personal pin in his posterior able to shake that conviction – he told Gordon Clough in January 1987 on the Radio 4 programme *The Press Barons*: 'I feel more at home with the Mirror Group than anywhere else. I love the smell of paper and ink, newly printed books . . . there's a nice feel about it.'

And behind the scenes, the Chairman would use me as a ploy in his business deals, though he never confided in me as to their details. To be honest, I wasn't particularly interested, anyway.

But when it came to wheeler-dealing, our party piece was rather good.

I would be invited to sit in on discussions, even if I was only half-listening. Sometimes in his office, but more often in a hotel suite.

At the crunch of the wheeler-dealing, the Chairman would lay his hand palm down on the desk, lean forward, and declare: 'Gentlemen, I view this proposal with such seriousness that I am going to ask my associate to leave the room.'

That was my cue to disappear.

Afterwards, with the deal completed, he would beckon me back. And explain: 'Mike, now you realise what a business ploy is all about. It makes the deal seem so much more important when I ask you to leave.'

'Fine with me, R.M.'

High finance wasn't my game, photography was. So who was I to argue?

But there was one occasion when I would have liked to stay. In the Presidential Suite of the Waldorf-Astoria in New York, an associate bounced in while I was chatting with the Cap'n.

In front of me, and without preamble, he said: 'How would you like to make $30,000,000 in one night, Bob?'

The Boss's eyes lit up. 'Tell me, Mister!'

Then he raised a hand. To me, he said: 'Mike, at this stage I have to ask you to leave the room.'

I did so without question and without resentment. But I never did find out how to make that much money in one night.

As I said, the Boss didn't take me into his confidence on such matters. And I knew better than to ask.

Wine breakages apart, one thing I omitted to confide to the Old Man was the time he became the subject of *This Is Your Life*. I was one of the chosen handful to hear about it weeks in advance, sworn to secrecy like everyone else, in the full knowledge that if word got out to Maxwell himself, the rug would be pulled and the programme ditched.

Date of transmission: 14 December 1988. Michael Aspel was the presenter, and the producer was Malcolm Morris. The catalyst they chose to put it all together was David Frost. The covert operation even had a code name: *The House!*

Aspel hit R.M. with the famous Red Book at a function room at the Commonwealth Institution in Kensington. We had persuaded Bob to be there on the pretext of being a VIP at an art exhibition, and we were standing around with Frostie sipping wine – when suddenly Aspel jumped out from behind a curtain, waving the book and shouting: 'Robert Maxwell, this is your life!'

It was rare to see the Chairman lost for words, but this was one of those times.

After the initial reaction (slack jaw and stutter) he recovered enough to beam benevolently and allow himself to be led outside to the waiting Rolls and the 20-minute trip to Teddington Studios. I was along not just for the ride, but to take pictures.

A lot of familiar faces came out of the woodwork that Thursday night to salute him. Frost wore a grin like a Cheshire cat. The entire family turned out.

Afterwards there was a party in the VIP suite looking out on to the Thames and the roaring weir by Teddington Lock. In the Rolls heading back to town, the star of the show gave me a sidelong glance.

Mother Theresa with Cap'n Bob.

'I suppose you were in on this, Michael?'
'What – me, R.M.?' I said, radiating innocence.
But I could tell he was pleased as Punch.

The most unusual visitor I remember seeing at Maxwell House was Mother Theresa.

She arrived in London with a mission: to see if she could open a refuge for the homeless in Surrey. Someone had pin-pointed a large house in Woking that was up for sale, and she was here to view it.

And she wanted Cap'n Bob to help.

Word of his efforts for charity had spread – even if the main charity was the *Robert Maxwell Appreciation Society*, with a membership of one.

But there was Mother Theresa in the foyer of Maxwell House, waiting to be shown up to the Tenth-Floor penthouse.

The first I had known about it was an urgent call on my direct line. 'Get over here, quick!' said one of Bob's aides.

I had met Mother Theresa once before, in Bombay when I was covering a royal tour. But I had forgotten just how tiny she was – and yet with such strength residing in this outwardly fragile, sparrow-like figure.

Up in the apartment, I performed the introductions. 'Mr Maxwell . . . Mother Theresa of Calcutta . . .'

They sat together on a sofa. Bob turned to her. 'May I say how much I admire all you have done. I will be happy to give you money for your latest project.'

Mother Theresa shook her head. 'No, Mr Maxwell,' she responded. 'Thank you, but I can't take your money.'

The Boss's eyebrows rose. This was a first.

'But I will accept any publicity you can give me in your newspapers.'

'Of course.' His Rolls-Royce was waiting downstairs to take us to view the house in Woking. But suddenly the Chairman had a bright idea. 'Let's try something different. My personal helicopter!'

'I've never travelled in a helicopter before, Mr Maxwell.'

'Well, Madam, there is always a first time. Now is your chance!'

And that was how I came to be sitting next to Mother Theresa in Charlie 2, buzzing over the rooftops of South London, with Bob's huge bulk in its usual place next to the pilot, front seat left.

I snapped a few pictures of her with headphones on, capturing the delight and surprise of a child with a new toy. One of those shots would win me an award.

We landed in the grounds of the house, a large Victorian pile in the stockbroker belt, and hastened inside. As we walked briskly across the lawn, I had an idea.

'I'll tell you what, Mother Theresa. I'd love to get a picture of you in prayer.'

'Oh – ?' she turned her wise, lined old face to me.

'Yes,' I pursued. 'When we get to a suitable place, would you consider . . .

Mother Theresa's first experience of a chopper.

you know . . . getting down on your knees for me? I'm sure it will help the cause!'

I have to say that despite her size, or lack of it, Mother Theresa does have enormous charisma. I felt the full impact of it as she turned her bright gaze upon me like a searchlight, and responded: 'Certainly not! I never pose for pictures.'

Then she relented. 'But I will say a few prayers while I'm walking around the building.'

I got the message, loud and clear. You might say almost heaven sent. It would be up to me to have my camera ready, and take whatever I could get.

Which is exactly what happened, as the Chairman ushered his diminutive companion around the rambling red-brick building which, as I recall, was being used as some kind of company office. He was unusually quiet, and I realised that this small person with us was one of the few people in whose presence even Cap'n Bob felt in awe.

Suddenly, with the sun flooding through a window to frame her like an angel, Mother Theresa stopped and stood stock-still. She closed her eyes,

Mother Theresa answers Mr Snapper's prayers!

folded her hands, and I saw her lips moving.

The picture made page one next day.

'Tell me, Michael,' the Chairman said later, pouring me a glass of celebratory champagne, 'did I really hear you ask Mother Theresa if she would pray for you?'

'Well, yes – in a manner of speaking, R. M.'

He banged the paper with a big, ebullient hand. 'Well, Mr Snapper, it looks like someone was listening!'

Cap'n Bob never minded me cashing in on the perks that went with being part of his inner circle. Especially if it benefited Mirror Group Newspapers.

A prime example was Frank Sinatra's farewell concert at the Royal Albert Hall. Ol' Blue Eyes was back for yet another final appearance, doing it his way.

Maxwell Communications Corporation kept a permanent option on a Box, all the year round, at a modest cost of £2,000. If we wanted to use it, we would have first bite. If not, the Albert Hall could offer it elsewhere.

The Old Man liked Sinatra, and not just because he had relieved the singer of $25,000 a day on the *Lady Ghislaine* for a week of fun and games in the West Indies. He liked the voice, he liked the music, and he had wooed Betty with Frank's inimitable tones warbling in the background.

This was going to be a great event, a hyped-up, sell-out concert with Frank's bosom buddies Sammy Davis Jnr and Liza Minnelli supporting the old guy.

Supporting in every sense, as it turned out.

Bob's P.A. Jean Baddeley suggested it would be a smashing idea to organise the Maxwell Hospitality Box for a few close friends, and the Boss willingly agreed. The maximum number would be eight. She invited the chairman of a bank, two leading City big-wigs, and an international industrialist.

There would be champagne, caviar and all the usual trimmings for which the Maxwell hospitality was renowned.

Photographs were strictly forbidden, and dire warnings circulated about what would happen to any photographer rash enough to try. Or, more to the point, to be caught trying.

I saw my chance.

Three days earlier, I made a recce of the place. Doing my homework, I bluffed my way in. 'I'm just checking out the Robert Maxwell Box.'

Of course, sir. Take your time.

I saw the problems at once. Box 91 was at least 200 feet from the stage. Frank Sinatra Junior would be conducting the orchestra while his old man was doing his stuff, and I would have to use a 600mm lens to capture the intimate moments.

A 600mm lens is at least three feet long.

So how to smuggle it in?

Problem number two: I couldn't set up a tripod in the box, because that would be too obvious. The solution was to use a monopod, a single-leg telescopic extension that could be lengthened to six feet in height. The light level would be low. I would have to shoot slowly $-1/_{30}$th of a second shutter speed, even with fast film.

I worked out a concealment plan worthy of Colditz. It was a black tie affair, certainly for those in the coveted Boxes. In my navy-blue BMW, parked a discreet distance from the Albert Hall, I pushed the monopod down my trouser leg. V-e-r-y carefully.

It meant that I couldn't bend my leg, so I had to walk with a limp. I put several rolls of film in my pockets. The 600mm lens lay along my arm, tucked under a raincoat, while I made sure I had the invitation in my other hand.

I was an hour early, but the crowds were flocking in and there was an excited buzz in the air.

A doorman eyed me as I hobbled gamely up the steps, swinging my stiff right leg like a war veteran.

'You're going to have a problem tonight, sir. The seats are very tight, and if you've got a bad leg –'

I waved my ticket in his face.

'Yes, I've broken it,' I said. 'But it's healing. Don't worry – I'm in a Box.'

'Oh, that's better, sir. You'll be okay. Just be careful as you go up the stairs.'

I was reminded of the climactic scenes in *The Day of the Jackal* as I limped heavily up the red carpeted staircase to the Boxes.

Inside Box 91, I shut the door, closed the burgundy curtains from the outside world, and moved fast. It took less than three minutes to assemble the equipment – camera on monopod, screw in lens, check film.

Then I shoved the whole lot under the table at the rear of the box. In darkness, no one could see it.

I pulled the curtains wide, took a deep breath, and surveyed the crowd below. Then I popped the bubbly.

Oh, what a night that was!

Only one person was missing from our illustrious Box – our host. He just didn't turn up. No explanation. No excuses. No phone call. No Cap'n Bob.

Which, for me, didn't matter one jot.

We knocked back the Dom Perignon '82, and the caviar, lobster and salad swiftly followed. By the time Ol' Blue Eyes strolled out on stage, Box 91 was feeling no pain and no strain.

We were on DP, Frank was on Jack Daniels. He actually had a full bottle of whisky beside the piano, and helped himself shamelessly and liberally throughout the next two unforgettable hours. He even drank it from a tumbler, neat.

He knew he was safe, because a whole posse of minders stood around, glowering at the audience, waiting for a flashbulb to go off. As someone remarked: 'He'd leave by the door – but they wouldn't bother to open it!'

But Frank hadn't reckoned with Mr Snapper.

Sinatra did a number. Liza did a number. Sammy did a number. Then they all three did a number. Then two of them sang, while the third wandered off into the wings – which, in the Albert Hall, is an opening past the orchestra.

Sinatra doing it his way.

It was brilliantly staged, and riveting from the first chord.

In the dim recesses of Box 91, Mr Snapper clicked away. None of our guests noticed, because I was shooting over their heads, using natural light. Sinatra began to wobble, and my camera picked out the tumbler in clear vision. Eventually, Liza would put a hand under each arm to hold him steady.

When I finished each roll I stuffed the film down the front of my trousers, inside my underpants, just in case.

Finally, Frank faced us with a full tumbler of Jack Daniels clutched in his hand.

'You killed my old man, but you ain't getting me!' he said to the glass. He drained it in one.

Then he sang the greatest version of *Strangers in the Night* I ever heard in my life.

Those pictures would make page one in *The People* on Sunday, and a two-page spread inside as well.

Afterwards, as I left with the monopod back in place down one leg, the lens under the raincoat over my arm, and an interesting bulge in the front of my trousers, the same attendant held the exit door open for me.

He asked anxiously: 'How was it, sir?'

With six rolls of film stuffed between my legs, there was only one answer.

'Painful,' I said.

And ol' watery eyes shuffled off into the night.

Another sell-out occasion where I was able to avail myself of the Chairman's perks happened on one of our trips to Japan. This time the superstar was Michael Jackson, no less, on the first concert of an 80-day world tour.

The *Mirror* knew I would be in Tokyo with the Chairman on one of his business trips, and managed to organise a Press ticket for me. When we got to Tokyo, I had an advance look at the great open-air stadium – and found that my worst fears were justified.

It would be night time. The drapes behind the stage were black. In their wisdom, the producers had decided to allow selected photographers to take their pictures of a black man (though admittedly Michael was going paler by the month) on a black stage – from 100 yards away.

It was going to be a circus, and for me a virtual waste of time. Two hundred photographers from across the globe had swarmed in to mark the great occasion. The organisers had put us all on an elevated stand where we could place our tripods, point them in the right direction, and hope for the best. Ludicrous!

In addition, we were only given two numbers to photograph the modern Messiah of Music before being ushered out. More ludicrous yet!

On the day before the concert, a ticket dropped into Cap'n Bob's pigeon-hole at the Imperial Hotel. Totally unexpected, a personal invitation from the Michael Jackson Management – and 12 rows from the front. Gratis.

In his suite, Bob was going through his mail. There were the usual invitations for an esteemed guest to cocktail parties and other social occasions. And one rather special invite.

He waved the ticket at me. 'What's this? Who's Michael Jackson?' he demanded.

I promise you, my esteemed Chairman really didn't know.

I tried to explain. 'He's one of the world's greatest entertainers, R.M. Remember the Jackson Five – ?'

'No!'

'Well, he sells more records than anyone else in the world – '

'Really?' The Chairman was supremely disinterested.

'Those tickets are like gold, R.M. – '

'Are they?' He looked down at the ticket, read it again – then threw it on the table.

'Well, Mr Snapper, go and do some panning!'

I slipped the ticket into my pocket, and knew I was in business.

One hour before the concert was due to begin we were all in place, as instructed on our Press tickets. Two hundred of us jostling for pole position, setting up our tripods, moaning about the hopeless conditions.

Suddenly – smoke, a thunder of drums, blaring music, and there he is . . . as the arena erupts and 120,000 screaming Japanese prove that they are not always so inscrutable, after all. A diminutive, strutting speck, though through the zoom lens he comes marginally into focus. I shoot off a few pictures.

End of second number. A posse of burly minders swing into action, escorting us down from our podium and waving us out into the night. But by now I have loaded my gear into a small bag, and seize the right moment at the height of the applause.

I slide away into the hysterical crowd, and head for the centre aisle, where the VIP seats are, waving my ticket at various attendants as Michael Jackson struts his stuff on the stage.

And there is the empty space, four seats in.

I wait for two more numbers, look casually around to confirm that the security guards are behind me, gazing intently out at the dense crowd for any flashlights or trouble – then fish into the case and bring out a 300mm lens.

When the deafening applause comes, that's when I start shooting.

There was no interval. Ninety minutes later I was up to my old trick of hiding the rolls of film in my underpants – trusting that no one was going to search me there – and making my slow exit.

Another page one spread was safely in the can.

Cap'n Bob scored a few own goals in his life, and risked another one when he was bitten by the bug of becoming a supremo of the soccer world. Being the man he was, he went charging down the pitch with all the enthusiasm of a schoolboy who has become hooked on Subbuteo – except that this was for real.

As the world knows, Bob bought Oxford United, then a lowly Third

'Do it this way, Elton'

Division club, in 1981, and started rattling cages. His much-publicised venture sparked a bolt of energy through the team – and indeed, its supporters. By December 1983 he had turned United's fortunes around from a loss of £156,354 to a modest but happy £28,286 profit in 18 months, and seen them surge triumphantly into Division One.

He also bought Derby County, bid for mighty Manchester United, and finally signed a contract with Elton John for Watford – only to have to tear up the £2,000,000 cheque amid much acrimony when the Football Association squashed the deal.

For myself, I got to know that Oxford pitch well. I have spent more time than most on touchlines from Walsall to Wembley, covered every F.A. Cup final in the past 20 years, and normally hope to be setting up my tripod on one of the glamour matches on a Saturday afternoon.

With Bob in the directors' box at Oxford United, I found myself huddled behind the goal at the Manor ground more often than I really wanted, but it went with the job.

The ground off Beech Road, incidentally, boasts the rare distinction of having the most irregular pitch in the country, with a seven-foot slope from corner to corner and four feet from side to side. But, as some wag remarked, since Cap'n Bob made a career of moving goalposts, he couldn't have wished for a better team!

I was never really sure whether the Old Man actually liked football, or even understood it. All right, he was photographed in his peaked cap in the black and gold Oxford colours cheering his team on from the directors' seats.

But the first frisson of doubt tickled my spine about his credibility as Chairman on the day I went with him into the dressing-room following Oxford's triumph in reaching the First Division.

'I must congratulate them,' the Chairman said, moving his bulk with remarkable rapidity down the tunnel from the pitch, with the roars from the terrace still ringing in his ears. I chased after him to get the vital pictures.

He had a bottle of champagne under his arm as he opened the dressing-room door without knocking, and barged straight in. Eleven exhausted players in various stages of getting ready for the bath looked up at the elephantine figure in their midst.

Bob started shaking hands.

'Congratulations . . . Well done, lads . . . I'm proud of you . . . Marvellous show . . . Let's crack this bottle . . . '

'Er – Chairman – ' I tugged on his sleeve, a rare gesture, I can assure you. 'R.M., please . . .'

'What is it? Where is your camera, Mister?'

'It's the wrong dressing-room, R.M. This is the Shrewsbury team! They lost – '

'What! Oh – ' Cap'n Bob looked around. His eye fell on the losing team's manager Chic Bates, who it later transpired had been in the middle of giving his boys a mammoth rollicking for having blown the game.

'Of course I know it's the wrong dressing-room.' Bob could never, ever, be seen to lose face. 'I just wanted to commiserate with them.'

He waved the bubbly at the bemused Bates.

'Better luck next time, then!'

And together we beat a hasty retreat.

But Cap'n Bob was always getting names, and not just dressing-rooms, mixed up. It was par for the course. He also tended to invade dressing-rooms *before* a match to gee up the team – whether they appreciated it or not.

One time I was with him when he bounced up to Peter Shilton, the England goalkeeper who had been a coup signing for Derby. Bob pumped the goalie's hand.

'I gather that you're a big cheese in this club,' he said jovially.

Shilton looked at his chairman in a slight daze.

'Huh?' he managed.

Bob thought he hadn't heard properly. 'I said: you're a big cheese, Mister. Ho, ho!' He laughed heartily.

Silence in the dressing-room.

On the way back to his seat, Bob muttered to me: 'That Stilton fellow didn't get it, did he?'

As I say, the Boss never was hot on names.

CHAPTER NINE

A Yen for the Orient

It was another mogul, the Hungarian-born film producer Alexander Korda, who once delivered a worthy piece of advice for anyone arriving penniless but bent on making his mark in big business in a strange city.

'You should march into the most expensive hotel in town, book the best suite, and start making phone calls!'

I often wondered whether Bob had read that little homily somewhere on his early climb up the ladder. Especially when, in the winter of 1989, we headed for the most expensive hotel – not just in town, but in the whole wide world. I am talking about the Imperial Hotel in Tokyo.

High above the snowbound wasteland of Siberia, we floated in a dark sky, taking the short route to Japan. Gulfstream 2 had refuelled at Moscow Airport, and taken off again immediately.

The reason for this trip, as far as I can ascertain, was to do some heavy business with leading Japanese industrialists, and discuss Pergamon's huge reservoir of books and learning manuals that lay in the vaults back in the U.K.

As a bonus, we would have an audience with the Japanese Deputy Prime Minister in person.

One of Cap'n Bob's less publicised sidelines was his post as Chairman of the Sasakawa Foundation 'to improve relations between Britain and Japan'. This trip would also take in Outer Mongolia and Korea. One of his subsidiary companies was marketing a revolutionary hi-tech language trainer, developed by Toshiba, which was no bigger than a walkman. But Bob had other raw fish to fry.

Suddenly Caroline the stewardess, appeared, visibly upset. We were tucking into our usual dinner of Beluga Caviar, chicken legs and smoked salmon, washed down with Dom Perignon. Nothing cooked. The days were long gone when Bob used to like his meals cooked on the plane.

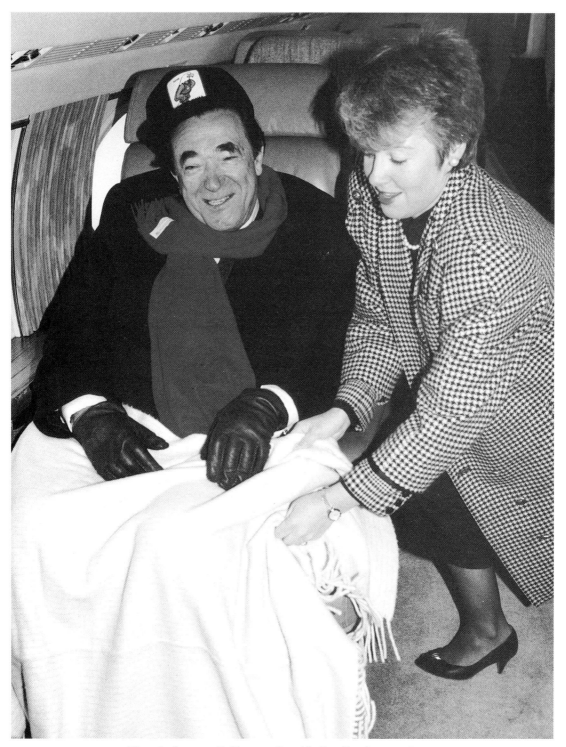

All tucked up on Gulfstream 2, with Caroline in attendance.

Also, I had discovered, the one thing he detested were fried onions – which for me was a crying shame, because I happen to like onions. Annoying, but I had to live with it. Now there was a cast-iron rule: no cooking on board Gulfstream 2 or Gulfstream 4.

Caroline hovered anxiously in front of us.

'Mr Maxwell,' she said hesitantly. 'I'm afraid I have some rather bad news for you.'

Bad news? Had someone passed out on the plane? Had Headington Hill Hall burned down? Had another Mirror Group editor resigned? Her expression was distraught.

Cap'n Bob bit heavily into his fifth chicken leg.

'What?' he growled. 'What's the problem?'

In hushed tones, the stewardess confided: 'I'm afraid you won't be able to use the toilet, Mr Maxwell.'

The Boss's brow darkened as he digested the implications, along with the chicken leg.

'Why?' The one word hung in the air like a thunder-cloud.

'I'm afraid it's blocked, Mr Maxwell,' she whispered, as if in a confessional. Poor kid, I thought, she's terribly embarrassed. Caroline was a nice, well-brought-up girl.

The Chairman reacted with typical aplomb. 'Who was the last person to have a shit in there?' he demanded.

He glared around. We shook our heads vigorously.

'Not me, R.M. . . . .'

'Nor me . . .'

The stewardess gulped, and went scarlet. 'Would you like me to close the toilet off, Mr Maxwell?'

'Certainly not.'

From the depths of his armchair, Cap'n Bob stirred. Slowly he rolled one sleeve up, then the other. 'Leave it to me!'

He pushed his tray away, rose ponderously to his feet, and strode past me aft to the curved loo door in the rear of the plane. His huge bulk disappeared from sight as the door partially closed behind him.

From inside the toilet strange sounds emanated, like a plumber's plunger working overtime.

Squish . . . squidge . . .

Squish . . . squidge . . .

I looked back. R.M.'s mighty pin-striped buttocks protruded through the door. He was on his knees, working away like a man possessed, the sounds coupled with heavy grunts. His right elbow rose and fell like a piston.

Squish . . . squidge . . .
Squish . . . squidge . . .
What on earth was he doing?
All too soon we found out.

Finally there was a horrid gurgling sound, like someone being sick. A jubilant Cap'n Bob appeared at the door of the loo, his face wreathed in smiles, his bare forearm hung with bits of green tissue paper and curious brown stains.

'There is no longer a problem,' he announced triumphantly. Wiping his forearm with a towel, he sank back into his seat to finish his dinner.

Outside the futuristic steel and glass arrival hall at Tokyo's Narita Airport, a cortege of sleek limousines awaited us. A reception committee of officials and executives from our Japanese office bowed and scraped dutifully in greeting to the Boss. To me, they all looked the same.

The Chairman made for the first car, a huge stretch Mercedes. He signalled for me to join him, waving the rest away to the other vehicles. Peter Jay, as Chief of Staff, was left to deal with the luggage – all 47 pieces of it. I thought that it would just about fit into a removal lorry!

We were heading for the Imperial Palace which, as I have said, renowned as the most expensive hotel in the whole world as befits the most expensive city. I settled back with the Cap'n, stretched my feet out, and prepared for a long journey into town.

A friend of mine who had made the same journey a month before had reported back that his taxi had cost him £100. But Bob wouldn't have been interested, so I didn't bother him with such incidentals.

Instead, we both became aware of an unexpected companion in our midst.

A young Japanese girl with exquisite features and with jet black hair trimmed into a neat bob was perched on the jump seat immediately opposite the Chairman.

She was wearing a crisp white orderly's coat, and there was a small surgical bag on the floor beside her.

We stared at her – and she bowed gracefully. Then, without a word, she bent and started to undo the Chairman's shoelaces.

Bob was startled. He looked at me, but I could only shake my head with a shrug. He glared at her.

'What are you to do with our party, madam?' he demanded.

'I am your massage, Maxwell-San,' the young beauty lisped, preparing to remove his shoes. And indeed she was.

Hello, I thought, remembering stories of what goes on in Tokyo's massage parlours. Our hosts are spreading out the welcome mat a trifle soon.

In fact, I was close to the truth. Mindful of the fact that that we had been in the air for close to 14 hours, our hosts had thoughtfully ordered a masseuse for the Chairman.

She took off his shoes and socks. A cheesy aroma filled the car, and I noticed steam rising from the Cap'n's size 12 feet. This was slightly surprising, becaues Bob was always fastidious about cleanliness. Indeed, he had changed his shirt three times on the flight. But perhaps changing socks isn't as easy when you weigh 20 stone.

Professional to the last, the girl remained inscrutable. She rubbed oil into his feet from a small bottle and began to massage him, toe by toe.

'What is your name, young lady?' Bob inquired benevolently. The foot massage was having its effect, even if the steam was still rising from the floor like Mount Fuji threatening to erupt.

In Japan they offer you their surname first when introduced, with the courtesy addition San. Bob was Maxwell-San. I became Maronie-San – they never could pronounce my name – 'But at least it's better than Macaroni,' I said to the Boss.

On meeting a newcomer, R.M. would always ask: 'What's your name, and what do you do?' Not because it was a way of breaking the ice – the Chairman normally crashed through any ice without giving it much notice – but because he just had to know your name and occupation.

Right now he knew what our companion did – but not her identity.

So – her name?

She looked up at him. Then said calmly: 'Oh fuck you!'

I had never seen the Chairman pole-axed. But then, I had never heard anyone address him like that. For myself, I knew Japanese women were becoming more liberated, but this was a bit much.

'*What!*' demanded Bob, his florid face darkening. '*What did you say?*'

'Is my name,' she repeated, wide-eyed. '*Ofuku!* It means Little Scented Flower.'

Not in this car, it doesn't, I thought grimly.

I looked at the Chairman, as a huge guffaw suddenly shook his frame. Bellows of laughter filled the car.

'Mike,' he said. 'I think we're going to enjoy Japan!'

Regularly on our travels I would sign the bills – after checking them closely. Bob entrusted me with some extraordinary responsibilities.

The ritual went like this: all the bookings would be organised by a firm based at Heathrow named MAMI (Marine Aircraft Management Incorporated). Plane, flight plans, number of passengers on board, transport at the other end, etc., etc. An extremely efficient outfit.

They would organise a 'bill back' facility which, as it indicates, meant that once the bill was signed it would be sent back to the Group Accounts for payment.

Frequently my job was to check the bill and put my signature to it.

I had my own personal 'Maxwell Expenses' account besides, which would be counter-signed by the Managing Editor himself, Ken Udall. There was never a single query.

But even after five years with the Maxwell Circus, I have to admit my jaw would sag after our sojourn at the Imperial. What we would spend in five days would buy a house in London – all £56,000 of it.

Mind you, it was a spectacular place. Outside in the courtyard fountains played, floodlit at night in the shape of rose-coloured triangles. Founded in the year 1890 'under the behest of the Imperial Palace', so the brochure told us, the hotel 'remains a legend close to the soul of the city of Tokyo'.

Inside the colonnaded marble foyer, we were bowed in by kimono-clad ladies, and checked in at a desk where every member of the staff spoke five languages.

Or, as the brochure put it: 'It is here, today, where over a century of experience in receiving special guests culminates in an elegant melange of exhilarating luxury, endearing personal service and rare epicurean pleasure. The Imperial awaits you with a world of beguiling, graceful precison and care . . . '

It also awaited our wallet.

Acting on Alexander Korda's advice, Bob had booked himself into the Imperial Suite. After all, he reasoned, status rather than stature is everything in Japan. Ronald Reagan, Margaret Thatcher, Mikhail Gorbachev and other Heads of State had all stayed there, and he was going to meet the Deputy Prime Minister anyway. So why go down market?

As Bob put it to me: 'Kings and Queens and Presidents stay here, so I have to.' He actually figured that it would be an insult to his hosts if he stayed anywhere else.

In other words, much loss of face.

The Imperial Suite cost 800,000 yen a night, without breakfast. Which at 210 yen to the pound didn't need an Einstein to work out the equivalent in sterling: close to £4,000.

At least I noted 'Baby crib free of charge'. If things got rough, I could always sleep in that, and Bob could rock me to shuteye.

In fact my own suite on the same floor as the Chairman's was exquisitely decorated in delicate shades of pastel, with a crisp cotton *yukata* kimono laid out on the bed next to the TV remote-control console.

I took another look at the brochure, and found that each suite and room was designed 'to compliment the prevailing ambiance of quality amidst posh tranquillity and quiet opulence'. Posh, it was. I could compliment them on that.

And who was I to correct their spelling?

While Bob was away, we played. Exploring the *Rainbow Room* with its 40 different international dishes lined up on the menu, the *Prunier* fish restaurant dating from 1934, and the *Kamon* – the *teppanyaki* dining-room for the local Nippon fare. I could live with that, too.

You will gather it was an arm, a leg and several other limbs to stay at the Imperial. Add to this the fact that no one ever really knew what Bob had ordered, especially when he was enjoying his beloved Dom Perignon champagne, and you can see how the bill would escalate.

In this case, out of sight.

A bottle of DP was £400 a time. The modest house wine was £75.

Ouch!

For the next three days the Boss was busy with his own affairs. This included setting up a joint world-wide news service with local media chief Yasudi Ogawa to spread the word on the latest Japanese technology. He also

Rival media moguls – but a personal handshake. Robert and Rupert meet in Tokyo.

signed a deal with Toshiba's Chief Executive Officer Joichi Aoi to market a compact language 'tutor' that would fit into the pockets of businessmen and students across the globe.

He even held a party for Japan's media elite, among them the aforesaid Mr Ogawa from Comline News Service, Mr Yosaji Kobayashi, president of Yomiuri – plus a surprise guest in the person of Rupert Murdoch, who just happened to be in Tokyo at the same time as our own delegation.

Contrary to what you may have read elsewhere, Robert Maxwell was not at daggers drawn with the infamously named 'Dirty Digger'. They might be arch-rivals in business, but they were still happy to chat over a glass of something chilled. In Rupert's case, tonic water. In Bob's, lager.

As the Boss put it to one interviewer: 'If the rivalry between Maxwell and Murdoch didn't exist, we'd have to invent it! You must assume that a lot of it is exaggerated.'

And to climax the trip: a meeting with the Deputy Prime Minister, Mr Shin Kamamura, who had just bought himself a new £130,000 black Bentley Turbo. I was listening when he told Bob: 'Now you see that Japan doesn't only export cars. We buy them as well.' This naturally called for a photograph of the

Mr Shin Kamamura, Japan's Deputy Prime Minister, poses by his new pride and joy, the £130,000 Bentley Turbo.

diminutive 74-year-old Liberal Democrat – even after Bob had told him sternly how to run his country.

'Time is running out for you.' I presumed he meant the country, not its aged deputy premier. 'It is not possible for Europe to have 30,000,000 unemployed while Japan exports its huge surplus and has no unemployment.'

The thinning-haired Mr Shin remained suitably impassive. And posed for my camera with arms folded, and with total lack of expression.

On the third day, Bob started getting grumpy. Jean, Debbie and I held a council of war, and came to the conclusion it was the food that was troubling him. Or the lack of it – the kind he really wanted.

We knew the telltale signs. The Boss was cheesed off, as simple as that. He was bored with raw fish and other Japanese delicacies, and even the myriad dishes that could have been ordered up to his suite from the *Rainbow Room* had ceased to excite him.

We had a word in his ear. There was a kitchen in the suite, tucked away off

Cap'n Bob with fellow Panda (stuffed), a present from his Nipponese hosts.

the main living-room area. Fine silver cutlery and bone china crockery in the drawers. As self-catering went, it was rather impressive.

'Why don't we go out and find you something you'll really like, R.M.?'

The Boss brightened.

'Good idea,' he said. 'How about a *smorgasbord*, or something.' Regularly back home in London at Maxwell House he would go to the kitchen, and help himself to chunks of ham and slices of cheese for an informal snack from the fridge. A few cold cuts would suit him fine.

So Jean, Debbie and I were despatched into the teeming streets, looking for unusual food.

We found what we wanted in a luxury delicatessen. Quails eggs – well, they were the Japanese equivalent, don't ask me what. And a type of smoked pork, beautifully wrapped, plus other delicacies to amuse the Chairman's palate.

In all, we spent £300 on it. Paid in yen, in cash, from a big wad I had been given for day-to-day expenses.

We brought the food back in triumph. Prepared it in the kitchen with fresh-baked bread, and bore it into the living-room with due ceremony at around five o'clock in the afternoon – a late lunch.

Bob eyed it appreciatively. 'That looks nice,' he said.

He sat down, unwrapped a crisp white napkin, jabbed a fork into the pink-edged slivers of smoked pork – and blanched.

'What the fuck's this?'

'What do you mean, R.M.? What's wrong with it?'

The Boss delivered the verdict of a Master Gourmet.

'It tastes like smoked camel's arseholes!'

Well, I have to say that both Jean and Debbie were visibly upset. They actually stormed out of the room, leaving the two of us together.

Bob looked at me, and suddenly broke out into a guffaw. He prodded the pork again. 'It even looks like it, Mister!'

But the ladies would get their own back.

In their own good time.

On the fourth day – great news! For me, anyway. A bonus arrived for Mr Snapper in the shape of a FAX from London. I had won an award – the Martini Royal Photographer of the Year.

'What was your photograph, Michael?' asked Bob, impressed despite himself.

'Actually, R.M., it's a picture of the Duchess of York crouched down for me so that she looks the same size as Ronnie Corbett,' I said.

'Who's Ronnie Corbett?' The Cap'n never did watch a lot of television.

My award-winning picture of Ronnie Corbett and Fergie. 'Who is Ronnie Corbett?' asked Cap'n Bob.

I told him, but I don't think he took it in. Instead he declared: 'We must celebrate this, Mike. Tonight!'

The Boss was in a good mood. He had spent the day with the man he had come to see, the small but financially perfectly formed (ie fabulously rich) Mr Ryoichi Sasakawa, who had already helped Bob bail out the Commonwealth Games with that donation of £2 million.

The good mood cost the Cap'n eight bottles of Dom Perignon, plus lashings of caviar, lobster canapes, the lot, sent up to the Imperial Suite for the entourage to quaff down on my behalf.

At the end, there wasn't a lot of change out of £4,000.

Five days later, as the Chairman and his entourage checked out, I went ahead to the foyer and asked for the bill for the Imperial Suite. I had my pocket calculator, and at 210 yen to the pound it didn't take me long to verify that the figures were correct. To this day, I remember the noughts: 11,760,000 yen isn't a figure you forget in a hurry – it equals £56,000.

Because I had to sign it.

Another big name that hove up on the horizon belonged to Henry Kissinger. On 2 December 1989, the legendary diplomatic Mr Fixit was invited by Cap'n Bob to breakfast with him in the Imperial Suite.

The phone in my own suite down the corridor rang at 6 a.m. My presence was required to photograph these two world figures – as Bob would like to think of Dr K. and himself – together over the croissants and coffee.

'Be here at 7.30 a.m.,' Maxwell's voice boomed down the line, jolting me into the land of the living.

Early start.

I shaved and showered, checked my cameras, and was about to head for the door when I stopped in my tracks.

From outside the windows came an unearthly sound like weird chanting, coupled with Japanese pop music blaring out from tannoys.

At 7.30 in the morning?

That was one they'd forgotten to include in the Imperial brochure.

My suite was on the same floor as R.M.'s. I slid open the doors, put my nose out on the balcony – and blinked. There, 20 floors down, was an incredible sight. At least 400 workers, identically dressed in white boilersuits and yellow hard hats, were limbering up for the day's work – indulging in collective callisthenics. They were in absolute unison – arms

High-level discussions with Henry Kissinger – over breakfast.

flailing, legs kicking and all to the shouted instructions of a leader conducting in time to the music, leading the chanting.

Their voices rose like an uncelestial choir to the heavens, in rhythm with their arms and legs.

'*Oi-yoo-ya! Oi-yoo-yah!*'

I shook my head in disbelief, and made my way to Bob's suite, knocked, and walked in.

Bob and Kissinger were sitting together on a sofa in front of a low table loaded with coffee and plates of croissants. They looked like two old friends getting together to talk over old times at a school reunion.

The noise from below filtered through the window.

Bob introduced me. 'Henry, I want you to meet the world's greatest photographer.' I'd heard that one before, and I wasn't going to deny it. 'Sit down, Mike, have some coffee.'

Neither of them got up, so I bent over to shake hands with Dr K.

'Can I just pose you here . . . ' I began – when the Chairman broke in.

'What the fuck's that noise?' he demanded.

The double-glazed windows were shut, but you couldn't help hearing the weird cacophony from below.

'I'll tell you what it is, R.M.,' I told him. 'It's a load of workers limbering up

Limbering up. Early morning work-out below Robert Maxwell's £4,000-a-night Presidential Suite at the Imperial Hotel.

before they start their day.'

The Chairman and Kissinger rose as one man, and went to the window. I joined them on the balcony. We gazed down at the bizarre spectacle below.

There was a long silence.

At last Maxwell said: 'Not a bad idea. Is it, Henry?'

'I don't think I'd go as far as that, Bob. You'd have a riot on your hands,' said Dr Kissinger. 'Right now I think I'll have some more coffee.'

On behalf of 5,000 *Mirror* employees, I'd say he deserved his Nobel prize.

From Tokyo we headed for Outer Mongolia, leaving Narita Airport at 2 p.m. with the nose of Gulfstream 4 pointed towards Ulan Bator, the capital of that far-off, mysterious country.

The call sign for G4 was VR-BOB. 'It stands for Very Rich Bob,' the Chairman once informed me with heavy humour when I asked him.

Into Outer Mongolia. The Gulfstream ensemble: left to right Mike, Debbie Dines, Capt John McCullen, R.M., co-pilot Brian Hull, Ian Maxwell, third pilot, Caroline the stewardess and Jean Baddeley.

We had a select party of seven on board. Cap'n Bob, Ian Maxwell, Andrea Martin (Bob's personal assistant), *Mirror* writer Nick Davies and Simon Grigg the butler (pronounced Grieg, as in composer). Also in the party was Lord Donough, a financial adviser who for reasons known only to himself and his host was along for the ride.

Two minutes after we took off, I peered out at the massive snow-covered slopes of Mount Fuji, which had notched up a remarkable number of unscheduled aircraft ploughing into its slopes. At 12,425 feet, it is the highest mountain in Japan, and something of a holy shrine as well as an early grave.

'I don't know whether you realise this, R.M.,' I remarked, sitting down in the seat across the aisle from him. 'But we are approaching one of the most spectacular volcanoes in the world. Wouldn't it be marvellous if we could get a shot of the crater?'

I paused, and added: 'But of course that's impossible.'

The word 'impossible' jolted Bob into action, as I knew it would. The proverbial red rag to a bull.

'Impossible? What do you mean, impossible?'

'I mean we'd have to fly over it.'

Immediately Bob reached up and prodded the call button to summon the stewardess – even though the 'Fasten Seat Belt' warning light was still on, and we were in a steep climb heading into the stratosphere.

Brave Caroline came lurching down the aisle, hanging on to the seat backs for dear life. Bob told her: 'Get me the Captain immediately!'

The plane started to level out. Now it was Captain Brian Hull who came stumbling out of the flight deck, straightening himself as best he could before the Chairman.

'Yes, sir? You wanted to see me?'

Bob looked up at him, then across at me.

'This photographic genius' – he pointed a stubby finger in my direction – 'wants a picture of the crater of Mount Fuji. Fly over it for him!'

The Captain's brow furrowed. 'We can't do that, Mr Maxwell. It's not on our flight plan.'

Bob's own brow darkened dangerously.

'Just fucking do it.'

The Captain did it.

We altered course and zoomed in low, looping around the great crater while I seized my camera and start clicking away.

Through the open door to the flight deck, I could hear the intercom crackling as Japanese ground control, who always play it inflexibly by the book, went noisily berserk.

Hon'ble VR-BOB getting much flak across the ether.

But I got my shots as the plane banked – and spectacular they turned out to be – a wondrous mixture of white snow, black rocks and grey steam hissing from the centre to create some extraordinary patterns. I could see another award looming on the horizon already!

The last time that volcano erupted was in 1707, so I reckoned we were fairly safe. But I also couldn't help a passing thought that if there had been an eruption we would have been blown out of the sky, and become another notch on Mount Fuji's impressive belt.

Three hours later we touched down in Seoul in South Korea, to refuel for Outer Mongolia.

From the air, Ulan Bator is a grey, blank, endless moonscape, with just one monolith disturbing it – a power station.

At the snow-packed airport we were greeted by a welcoming party of Mongolians wrapped in furs against the biting cold, led by the personal ADC to Mr Batmunkh, head of the government of the People's Republic of Outer Mongolia.

Bob wore a Russian fur hat with ear flaps, and we were each presented with a scarf fashioned from the renowned Mongolian cashmere. Its neutral shade of brown and grey merged nicely with the landscape.

Why a scarf? I recalled somewhere that Bob had talked about tying up a deal to export cashmere to the West.

'Mister,' queried Bob, as we crunched over the hard-packed snow to the glass doors of the arrival hall, 'is this your first trip to Mongolia?'

'Yes it is, R.M.,' I said.

'Well, make sure it's your last,' he said. 'And let me give you a tip. Watch out for the yak shit!'

As we approached the primitive terminal, I felt a nudge in my ribs. 'That's no way for the Chairman to refer to the President of Israel,' muttered one of our party, with a discreet smirk. Sorry, Yitshak Shamir!

For once, no fleet of limousines was awaiting us. Instead, just a battered old Dormobile for the Chairman and the ADC. And for us – a filthy, mud-spattered bus that had seen better days several decades ago.

Our two-strong convoy bumped along badly made roads, avoiding potholes, through a cheerless landscape that made me think of Neil Armstrong's first big step for mankind. On either side of the road were clusters of tents, and I glimpsed fur-hatted figures grouped around small fires, warming their hands against the cold.

The British Embassy was a welcome oasis in this alien wilderness, and our whole party would be staying there for just one night. Quite what Our Man had made of his furlough in this lost land, I could not imagine.

Ulan Bator seemed like nothing more than a cluster of ill-lit streets and mud huts roughly half the size of your average market town in Sussex or Shropshire. As we bumped and trundled up to the official residence, I was reminded of a second-class hotel in Clacton.

Our Man in Mongolia opened the front door himself. He turned out to be a surprisingly youthful figure who could well have been the headmaster of a top public school. His Excellency Guy Hart OBE was a career diplomat who had been educated at Cranleigh and come up in the ranks through the Intelligence Corps.

His wife Elizabeth stood beside him, elegant and refined as behoves the First Lady representing her country in a foreign land. She extended a slim hand to each of us in turn as we stepped over the threshold.

'Good afternoon, Mr Maxwell,' she said to our leader. 'Welcome to Mongolia.'

To which the Chairman summoned his wealth of wit and wisdom in response.

'Madame Ambassador. This must be the arsehole of the world!'

Madame Ambassador lifted one eyebrow a fraction. Her gaze fastened on a spot a foot above Cap'n Bob's shoulder.

'Tea is being served in the drawing-room. Would you care to follow me?'

If there was a hint of frost in the air, ebullient Cap'n Bob failed to notice it.

The interior of the Official Residence was more YMCA than Clacton, and the surroundings were, to say the least, basic. We all had to double up, with the exception of Cap'n Bob, who had the main guest room – indeed, the only guest room – in the building.

We stayed for just the one night, but it was enough. Social life in Ulan Bator seemed to be in decline, and the joint wasn't exactly jumping.

But next day, at least, we had an audience with the head man, a small, impressive figure with silvering sideburns and a cool but pleasant enough manner. Mr Janbyn Batmunkh held the title of Head of the Government of the People's Republic of Outer Mongolia, which presumably meant that he carried a certain clout on his home ground.

I had no idea what we were doing there in Outer Mongolia. To this day, I still don't know. But I went along with the Chairman in our battered VIP transport to the Imperial Palace. And duly posed him with his host under a painting of King Chengis-Han, the 13th-century 'revered founder' of Mongolia, which decorated the otherwise sparse and functional main office.

The revered founder stared balefully out from the canvas, black-bearded

'The arsehole of the world!' Cap'n Bob's own words. But not when he met the President of Outer Mongolia.

and black-garbed, and for no reason at all it occurred to me that he would have been 700 years old if he had survived to this day.

Mission over. The Boss appeared pleased.

A farewell wave from Our Man in Outer Mongolia and his delightful lady, and our mini-cavalcade rumbled off through the potholes to the airport. None of us could wait to get out of the place, and a new air of levity pervaded the jet.

The girls had been simmering quietly ever since the incident with the *smorgasbord* in Tokyo. Now they hatched their revenge, aided by Caroline the stewardess who was brought in on the act.

In the galley of the Gulfstream, Jean and Debbie prepared another feast for the Chairman, similar to the one over which we had all taken such trouble at the hotel. But this time they sprinkled the plate with chocolate drops, long red strips of frankfurter, wrinkled squares of ham that were going to be thrown out

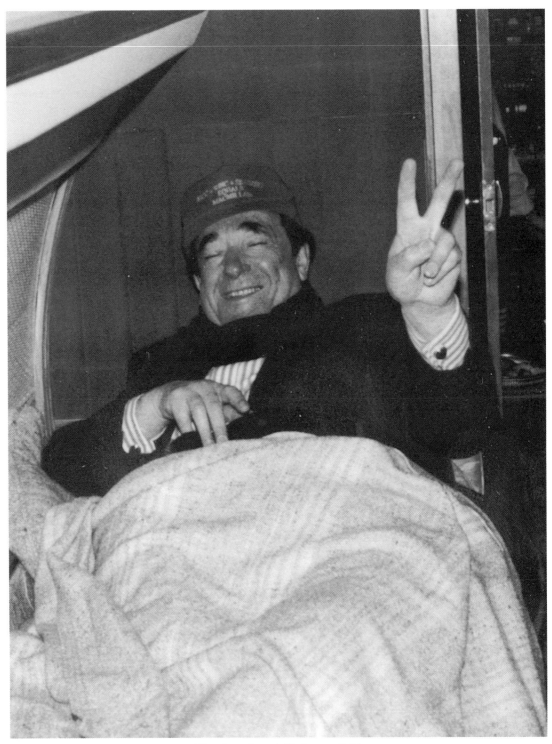

The thoughts of Chairman Bob!

anyway, and baked beans. Finally they squirted Fairy Liquid over the top.

Then the three of us marched down the aisle to the Boss.

'Mr Maxwell,' said Debbie, placing the tray in front of him, 'can we present you with this?'

The Chairman looked down at the grisly offering under its coating of green slime.

'What's all this?'

'This is smoked camel's arseholes!' we chorused in joyous unison.

The Boss just looked at us, then retreated behind his paper without a word – or a smile.

CHAPTER TEN

Dr Dolittle Lives!

Kenya, October 1986. We were guests of the President of Kenya, one Daniel arap Moi. Bob immediately dubbed him 'Danny Boy Moi', though naturally out of hearing of the Presidential ear.

The reason for the trip became apparent weeks later when a new version of the *Kenya Times* burst on to the streets of Nairobi. The headline across the centre-spread was the one word S-E-X in giant 180-point capitals. The story was about a university warden's concern over hanky-panky among his students. And a picture of two girls – one black, one white – in bikinis showed the deft hand of the *Mirror* behind it.

If anyone was in doubt, a photograph taking up a lot of space on page one showed President Moi with a familiar figure standing beside him, smiling broadly.

Who else but Cap'n Bob?

A deal had been struck. A big deal – the result of our sortie down to the Dark Continent in Gulfstream 2. Our intrepid team of explorers comprised Peter Jay, Jean Baddeley, the boss's secretary Debbie Dines and myself, plus camera bag.

Up until then, following the passing of the ostentatious Jomo Kenyatta (complete with fly-whisk, as I recall), the *Kenya Times* had been a dull, sycophantic and virtually unreadable daily tome reflecting the voice of government and precious little else.

The ruling KANU party had taken it over from its African publisher Hilary Ng'weno in 1983, at which time it was popular, dared to criticise the government, and made precious little profit.

The even heavier losses sustained under KANU didn't matter too much, since the less-than-vital organ was now an instrument of the State, and above such irritants as a balance sheet.

Until Chairman Maxwell cast his eye on it.

In two days of heavy talking he wrapped up the operation. 'My aim is to make the *Kenya Times* the most successful paper in all of East Africa, Mr President,' he solemnly informed Mr Moi at a reception at Government House to celebrate the signatures and the handshakes.

It transpired that Mirror Group Newspapers had taken out a 45 per cent stake in the *Times* through a new company called the Kenya Times Media Trust, with KANU retaining the other 55 per cent.

I can only say that Bob was like a prospector who had unearthed the Golden Nugget. I had seldom seen him so elated. He recognised the possibilites in his grasp, courtesy of his new-found friend in Government House.

Danny Boy could hand him the keys to the kingdom of the entire East African coastline.

Bob's emotions in that remarkable week were akin to those of Livingstone stumbling on the Zambezi in 1851, and setting his eyes on the Victoria Falls ('The Smoke that Thunders') for the first time four years later.

Otherwise, surely, the Cap'n would not have behaved quite so rashly as he did when he metamorphosed into the Great White Hunter and headed out into the Bush in search of other game – with me in attendance.

In those two heady days in Nairobi, the Chairman would invest funds into a 30-storey twin tower block in the heart of the capital, install a new full-colour printing works nearby, and also install the recent *Mirror* editor Mike Molloy on the board of directors.

Behind all this lay a deal to handle a 'wide range of printing, publishing and communications ventures', including the sole contract to print all text-books for the country's schools. Clever stuff. Massive potential.

Some doubting Thomases shook their heads in disbelief – as they often did when Bob went ballistic. The Kenyan currency was in a downward spiral, with its poor shilling getting a fresh hammering by the week. The aroma of devaluation lingered in the air like poison gas. Africa was then, and remains now, a notoriously volatile continent.

But Bob would have none of it. The first issue on 15 February the following year would trumpet the headline: TODAY A DREAM COMES TRUE! It added for good measure, and penned in the new Publisher's own choice words: 'Our ideas coincided so harmoniously that His Excellency felt justified in taking us into immediate partnership with KANU.'

That, together with the photo of Bob with Danny Boy, clinched it. 'Our venture is the first to gain Government approval under new regulations encouraging foreign investment,' Maxwell wrote, dangling the tempting carrot for the International Market.

As for the *Times*, it became the Dark Continent's version of the *Mirror*.

Eventually, sure enough, it would climb back into profit.

A new problem page featured its own black agony aunt named Sally – clad in a headscarf, Africa's answer to Claire Rayner.

For the record, her first problem letter dealt with a distraught grandmother whose 19-year-old treasure had left home to live with 'a layabout who wears an ear-ring.'

To some cynics, this suggested the unthinkable – that the letter had been invented. 'Ear-ringed layabouts are not yet one of Kenya's urban problems,' observed one commentator. 'It is more likely the poor girl has been abducted into a Masai village.' Something that dear Claire never had to face.

That first issue also produced some curious advice on food. An athletic white woman in a leotard was pictured enthusiastically swinging a pair of dumbbells to promote health and happiness. More dumbfounded, surely, were the readers who were advised to eat wholewheat toast and yoghurt, and sample low-calorie soup. None of which was available in Kenya.

Cap'n Bob had done it again, rushing in where wiser men feared to tread.

But that was for the future. For now, excitement was on the menu.

In the euphoria of those early spring days in another hemisphere it was time for rest and relaxation. We had been staying in the Mount Kenya Safari Club in Nairobi, a luxury urban watering-hole in the heart of the city.

When we arrived at the reception desk, an area surrounded by bamboo and foliage, they presented us with a hand-embroidered blazer badge, which I still sport proudly on special occasions, i.e., when I want to impress people. Two elephants' heads in silver, and Mt Kilimanjaro in the background. It's a conversation piece whenever I wear it.

But it was time to explore further afield. The President recommended Governor's Camp, a remote lodge buried deep in the Bush.

For transport, we were spoiled for choice. At Nairobi Airport, Gulfstream 2 sat waiting, ready to respond to the Chairman's every whim.

But Danny Boy Moi had other ideas. 'I would invite you and your party to take my own private plane,' he insisted, as we stood in a group together on the terrace of the Presidential Palace, sipping traditional sundowners of Brandy Sour.

I was pleasantly surprised. Up to then I had found him an unpleasant looking, even frightening figure, like so many African dictators, devoid of both charm and charisma.

Perhaps I had misjudged him.

'Mr Maxwell, I insist.'

Cap'n Bob bowed gratefully. 'Thank you, Mr President. You are very generous.'

As we walked down the marble steps to the waiting limousines to take us back to the Safari Park Hotel for the night, he muttered to me out of the corner of his mouth: 'Why waste my fuel?'

The Governor's Camp was an hour's flight, 300 miles away over the veldt. We took off at 5 a.m. for the dawn run. It was my first time in Kenya, and I stared down in endless fascination as the contours of this great land unrolled beneath us.

On safari at the Governor's Camp, Kenya.

No wonder this second largest continent after Asia had proved such a magnet for the likes of Richard Francis Burton and John Hanning Speke, Samuel Baker, James Grant, David Livingstone and Henry Morton Stanley, the sailor-turned-journalist who was actually a Welshman named Rowlands.

The Governor's Lodge had achieved its own place in history as the spot where Princess Elizabeth and Prince Philip spent the first happy days of their visit to Kenya in 1952, before moving on to Treetops where the tragic news of her father's death was broken to them.

For us, this was 'R and R' time, and Cap'n Bob rose to the occasion. A warden named Sam was assigned to escort us out to the wilds, a youthful veteran of the veldt in crisp khaki uniform that somehow never seemed to get creased.

Piled into a canvas-covered four-wheel-drive Land Rover with the sides rolled up, we set out to explore.

'Make sure your cameras are ready, Mike!' the Boss said. 'I don't want you to miss anything.'

'I won't, R.M.,' I assured our intrepid leader.

He certainly looked the part. Khaki fatigues, high boots to protect his ankles against snakes and scorpions, and a Bush hat to protect his head against the sun's glare.

'I've talked to the animals!'

Bob's first encounter with the big game denizens of Africa could have been his last. Bouncing along in the back of the Land Rover, peering eagerly out at the passing scenery of scrub, rocks and plane trees, we searched for a sight of something moving.

'Look, sah!'

Up front with the driver, Sam pointed to the left. I couldn't help noticing that our guardian had a .303 rifle across his lap, and that his right hand was hovering near the trigger.

'What?' We all craned to look.

There beside the track was a pride of lions. Half a dozen lean brown shapes lolling under a tree, totally ignoring the intruders – until the Land Rover came to a grinding halt ten yards away, on Bob's orders.

'Stop the Jeep!' he commanded. 'I want a closer look.' He eased his huge bulk towards the back of the Land Rover.

Sam looked panic-stricken 'No! Mr Maxwell-sah, please don't even consider getting out of the vehicle.'

'I have a way with animals, Mister!'

And the would-be Dr Dolittle of the Wilds poked a large head out of the rear, and made to alight.

'No, sah!' Our guide's voice rose an octave. 'No one has a way with these animals. They are very dangerous. Please – '

'I do,' said the Cap'n.

Impasse.

While the argument was going on, I decided it was time to get some pictures.

The best vantage point – and surely, the safest – was the roof of the vehicle. I clambered up behind the driver, on to the taut canvas roof. And kneeling there, focused my 300mm telephoto lens on the lions for some marvellous portraiture.

In close-up, through the lens, I saw a wonderful sight. Three lionesses – and with them, five cubs I hadn't noticed making up the family, bouncing out playfully from behind the rocks.

I could hear Bob growling his displeasure from inside the Land Rover – and then I heard another, different growl. A low, throaty snarl.

Behind you!

That was when I realised something was missing from this delightful family portrait. You've guessed it – the King of the Jungle himself.

I looked round for the source of the snarl – and went cold. Just a few feet away, on the far side of the Land Rover, unnoticed by any of us and within easy springing distance, crouched a lion that made Elsa look like a kitten. The

Heading for the vulture tree.

yellow eyes were fixed on me. It had come round unseen from the rear. Stalking us.

Now I have been told that lions can't smell humans if they (the humans) are in a vehicle, because the petrol or diesel fumes are too strong. At that moment I wasn't willing to take the chance.

Now, I thought, I know why big-game hunters wear khaki! All that was missing was the bicycle clips!

The altercation was still raging inside as slowly, ever so slowly, I edged back off the roof.

The Great White Hunter was declaring: 'I'll be all right. I know what I'm doing.'

'No, sah. It really is too dangerous.'

I slid into the interior. 'R.M.,' I said. 'Take a look out of the other side. Away from the cubs.'

He did, and there was a long pause.

Then the Boss nodded, slowly. 'Maybe you're right, Mister,' he said. 'Let's go on.'

The yellow eyes watched us depart, and I felt rivulets of sweat running down my back.

Silly, really. They can't smell us, can they?

During the next three hours, Africa put on her finest show. Game paraded past us like a scene from a nature trail. Zebra, giraffe, even a wart-hog, wildebeeste, hippos wallowing in the mud.

'What's that?' Bob asked once, gesturing at the long grass.

'A secretary bird, sah.'

'Ah, we'll call it Debbie,' said the Chairman, exhibiting his well-known wit.

In the middle of an empty plain, I saw a single tree growing like a thin bone out of the ground, with ominous grey shapes clustered in the branches.

'What are those?'

'Those, Mr Maxwell, are vultures.'

'Do they come from the Midland Bank?' queried the Chairman, by now in top form.

This time Sam did not protest when he insisted on stopping for a closer look. He walked over to them, and stared up at the tree. I snapped a few pictures.

'Nasty creatures,' said Sam to me. 'They pick over the bones.'

They've recognised a friend, I thought. To myself, naturally.

Suddenly the Land Rover veered to a stop. We craned around until our necks were aching. What was it?

Rhino!

'There!' Sam pointed through a clump of trees.

As any tourist will tell you who has been fortunate enough to experience a safari, the first sight of a rhinoceros is something they never, ever forget. The mammoth beasts, clad in the armour that has protected them for centuries, are like veterans from a prehistoric age. Maybe they are. My natural history isn't that brilliant. But in the middle of the African Bush, one to one with a great

One heavyweight meets another.

grey shape looming out of nowhere, it doesn't have to be.

The thing was enormous, somehow beautiful in its sheer ugliness, built like a Sherman tank. It rooted and snuffled at the grass as we approached. I did know that they are, in fact, herbivorous. I also knew that they are extremely short-sighted, and prone to charge anything that moves rather than get 20-20 vision on it.

Which is why we stayed absolutely still, with the engine turned off, in a silence that stretched to the far horizon.

'Cap'n Bob, I presume?' Mr Snapper with the great explorer.

We could hear the rhino grazing.

Chomp! Chomp!

'Isn't he incredible!' Jean whispered.

We nodded in unison. We had to agree, he was.

That was the moment the Boss decided to play Dr Dolittle again. And this time, Sam's protestations were in vain.

'I must get a closer look!' And he was out of the vehicle before anyone could stop him, and striding through the grass towards the massive beast.

'Sah! Sah!' Sam's shouts went unheeded.

In the cause of duty, I got out too, levelling my camera to capture the scene.

'Hold it right there, R.M.' I fired off a salvo of snaps.

That's when I saw the rhino lift its head, and turn its little piggy eyes in our direction. That beast, wonderful as he was, could turn our Land Rover over like a matchbox.

It was time for discretion to take the better part of valour. I heaved myself back inside, and looked back.

The rhino had turned, and was starting to trot towards the intruders, dust scuffing up from under its hooves. Not a charge, more curiosity – but exuding menace in every step.

Thank God, Cap'n Bob took the hint too, doubtless recognising an even greater heavyweight than himself.

His bulk surged back with surprising speed, and breathing heavily he scrambled back aboard as the driver put his foot on the pedal and accelerated away.

The great grey shape dwindled in the distance, staring after us.

For some reason I was reminded of the old circus joke where the novice lion-tamer is advised to pick up a handful of shit and throw it at the charging animal.

'Will there be any shit?' he queries.

'*Will there be any!*' says the trainer.

Flying back to Nairobi on the Presidential jet an hour later, Bob turned a beaming face to me.

'I told you I had a way with animals, Mike,' he said.

Over the years I flew high, wide and handsome with Cap'n Bob. In those champagne days, it seemed that the Heads of State of the entire world were queueing to be given a date in his diary.

For instance: October 1989.

Bob had been invited by Carlos Menem, President of Argentina, to be his house guest for five days in Buenos Aires. Another deal was in the offing.

I knew nothing about it until the morning of 17 October, with a phone call to my home from the Ninth Floor.

Get packed for warm weather. You're going to Argentina. And take your dinner jacket. First stop is New York.

No more explanations, but by now I didn't expect any. The Boss was already in New York, courtesy of Gulfstream 4, and I flew out to join him on Flight BA 177, Club Class.

I missed the lobster claws and caviar. But then, I figured, you can't have everything! And I was genuinely excited about the prospect of seeing South America for the first time.

At Kennedy Airport I was back in more familiar territory: greeted by a massive stretch limo with chauffeur attached. Ending up at the Hemsley Palace Hotel and a suite one floor below the penthouse where the Chairman was ensconced.

Cap'n Bob was in his element, holding court to an assortment of genuflecting courtiers, the needy and the greedy, all bowing obeisance to the Master and all with a favour to ask or a deal to be struck.

The only thing missing was the kneeling mat, I couldn't help thinking, as Bob immediately appointed me his meeter and greeter at the penthouse door. Or maybe a prayer mat for those in special need.

'Just get their names, Mike. That's all I need,' the Boss ordered. 'Keep them in the ante room for a couple of minutes, then I'll be ready for them.'

Maxwell was a walking anachronism. A man in his own time warp. He forgot names – even mine. He had never heard of Michael Jackson, who had taken up more ink in his own newspapers than most other stars combined. Sometimes I wondered if we were walking on the same planet. *Beam me up, Bob!*

But when it came to business, his mind was like a rat-trap. Sharp, incisive, asking the right questions and getting answers.

He had his own little homilies that he would deliver to me as if Moses himself had brought them down from the Mount.

'Never try to sell the skin until you've caught the rabbit, Michael!'

Whatever that meant.

'Yes, R.M. I mean – no, R.M.'

If that meant dealing with funds that you haven't actually got in place – oops!

At the Hemsley Palace, I became meeter and greeter to the likes of Henry Kissinger and assorted politicians. I was starting to look on Kissinger as something of an uncle figure, because I kept bumping into him to photograph him with my boss.

New York, with Ronald Reagan.

After two hours of it we set out for a banquet at the Grand Plaza Hotel, hosted by the President of the United States and actor turned statesman, Ronald Reagan.

I stood beside Cap'n Bob as he pumped the Presidential hand in the reception room where they served pre-dinner cocktails. Afterwards I noted Reagan examining his fingers.

'Say, Bob, that's a very strong grip you've got,' he said with that peculiarly soft and much imitated drawl. 'But – ' he lowered his voice, 'I've got to tell you something – '

'What's that, Mr President?'

'Your fly is undone.'

It was, too, and not for the first time. Bob's zip had a tendency to follow the force of gravity. I had seen it several times in decline, even if Reagan had never had the privilege.

But the Cap'n was equal to the occasion.

'Mr President,' he said, with heavy jocularity, 'don't worry. Dead birds don't fly!'

Reagan grinned his famous lop-sided cowboy smile. Thus giving the Chairman his chance to regale him with the only joke I ever heard him tell.

'Do you know, Mr President, someone once asked me: "What do you think would have been the world-wide implications if Kruschev had been assassinated – and not Jack Kennedy?"'

Now Reagan did look baffled. He shrugged his big shoulders.

'I'm sure I don't know, Bob!'

Maxwell's own shoulders heaved with anticipation of his punchline.

'I'm quite sure that Aristotle Onassis would not have married Mrs Kruschev!'

Sometimes my Chairman could be genuinely funny.

Ronnie shook his head. 'Gee, Bob, you're a real card!' No doubt meaning the joker in the pack. Laughter all round, accompanied by much back-slapping, as they headed together towards the dinner.

I couldn't help thinking: *vaudeville isn't dead yet.*

Once again, Bob followed his usual procedure, and left early. We managed to take in the main course of roast guinea fowl before the Chairman opposite me suddenly rose to his feet and lumbered for the door.

That was the signal for the rest of us to follow.

But this time there was a genuine reason for Bob to make his excuses and leave. Or, to be more accurate, to leave without any excuses at all.

He had a flight to catch.

All the way to Buenos Aires.

Gulfstream 4 was waiting at White Plains Airport, a 30-minute fast drive from the Grand Plaza.

We had until 11 p.m. to beat the deadline. For some reason, presumably because of noise control over the area, we had to be up, up and away by that time. Fair enough. Rules are rules, and I always maintain that noise is the eighth deadly sin, anyway.

We made it with minutes to spare. The plane took off, and once we were in the air we changed from our suits into casual gear. In Cap'n Bob's case, a voluminous grey track suit.

'Whoever would have thought a B-movie star could become President of the United States!' The Chairman eased his bulk into his own armchair, in pole position opposite his bed at the front of the plane, relaxing at last. 'But then, you could say the same for a peanut farmer!'

We all chuckled obligingly at his reference to Jimmy Carter.

The Boss looked around and extended his formal invitation for us to dine with him again.

'What about some camel's arsehole?'

That meant food, by now a regular reference to our spot of fun in Japan. So ... less than an hour after we had been tucking into roast guinea fowl with all the trimmings, we were off again!

Out came the familiar tray of smoked salmon, smoked ham, lobster claws and the inevitable Beluga, served by our darling Caroline, the ever-smiling stewardess. How she kept up that smile I'll never know.

Bob tucked in with relish. I stayed with the Beluga, and the deep-chilled vodka which had by now become my favourite too.

Finally, in the early hours, lights out! Time for sleep.

I settled back in my armchair in the cabin behind the Chairman's private quarters, put a mask over my eyes, and dozed off, letting the subdued roar of the Gulfstream's twin jets lull me into dreamland. It had been a long night.

Two hours later, I felt a nudge on my knee.

I woke to find Cap'n Bob towering over me.

'Do you fancy a swim, Mister?' This time, meant not unkindly.

His booming voice filled the cabin.

I blinked back into the real world. Or should that read surreal? But managed a rather smart riposte.

'Don't tell me, Chairman. You've got a pool on the plane!'

He liked that, and bellows of merriment woke anyone else who had managed to stay asleep so far.

'No, Mike. I thought we might stop in Rio on the way down.'

'Brilliant idea, R.M.' I was tired, disorientated, freshly disturbed from sleep, and what else could I say? Later, in fact, I thought it was a good idea. We might even meet Ronnie Biggs down there. That would be a great picture. Two seasoned rogues in one frame!

Bob put his head into the flight deck, and issued instructions. 'Copacabana, and make it quick!' ordered the Chairman. 'I fancy a swim.'

You don't often hear throwaway lines like that.

Landing permission obtained. The Gulfstream soared down over Sugar Loaf Mountain. I caught a glimpse of Corvocado Peak, with its colossal statue of Christ which from the air looked like a tiny monument, brilliantly lit by the first rays of the sun.

Somehow, two limousines had been spirited from nowhere, and were waiting for us in the early dawn.

And there on the famous Copacabana Beach, the Cap'n rolled up his trousers and went for a paddle in the surf.

'I am King Canute!' he declared to the world at large – consisting at that hour of two small barefoot urchins in torn jeans squatting in the sand.

King Canute steps out.

King Bob was in playful mood.

'I can do anything. I can order the waves back!'

He took off his shoes and socks, rolled his trousers up to his knees, and strode into the briny. The Atlantic thought otherwise. Responding with a mighty wave that soaked him from head to toe.

I have to admit that, somewhat unfortunately, my picture makes it look as if my Chairman was having a piddle rather than a paddle. But, for the record, not so.

Wiping himself down, Cap'n Bob retreated back to the safety of the sand.

'There, Michael. You've got what you're always after. A page one splash!'

And, dripping, his huge frame heaved with laughter.

On down to Buenos Aires to meet President Carlos Menem, who else?

But first, a dinner in Bob's honour to welcome *el Capitano* to Argentina, held with due ceremony at the magnificent private house of a businessman whose name I never did discover, but whose hospitality I was happy to accept.

Ten of us around a long table with silver candelabra under gleaming chandeliers, tucking into wonderful beef – what else?

I noticed that Bob had been positioned at the far end, between two well-dressed and eminent looking men I judged to be in their 50s, and was engrossed in conversation with them. I had seldom seen the Boss so intent.

'Who are those gentlemen, may I ask?' I said to one of our hosts next to me.

'Ah, they are plastic surgeons,' my neighbour responded. 'Two of our leading experts in that field. Senor Maxwell particularly asked to meet them. So – it was arranged.'

Oh? I said. And thought no more of it.

Except to note that the Old Man stayed later than usual, talking to his new *compadres*.

Next day, we drove out from our hotel in a fleet of limousines to the Presidential country retreat located 30 miles outside the city.

My first impression was of high walls topped with razor-wire, electronic alarms, armed guards and massive security. My second impression, after we were driven up to a stylish hacienda-type house with red tiles and balconies, was of two figures kicking a football at one another on the lawn, one of whom was immediately familiar.

Pele, no less! The mighty Brazilian soccer ace was performing his usual magic, happily showing off by bouncing the ball on his foot, his knee, his head and back to his boot again, before returning the pass.

The other man was the President of Argentina himself!

Introductions all round. I had met Pele once before, in London, so I took it

J.C., R.M., M.M.

Rio: Bob with Andrea Martin.

on myself to introduce him to the Cap'n. By now, Maxwell had transferred his interest in Oxford United to his son Kevin, and taken on Derby County as his pet team.

'Of course, Chairman, this gentleman needs no introduction – ' I gestured at the soccer legend.

Bob looked blank.

'Er – this is Pele, R.M.. One of the greatest footballers I have ever seen – '

'Umm,' said Bob. 'Well, if you're that good, Mister, maybe you should come and play for Derby.'

Pele, who doesn't speak a great deal of English, nodded in bemusement. He was running late, and couldn't stop for more than that exchange.

Up came Carlos, with a hand extended, and an invitation to join him for coffee. Before we went inside, I persuaded them to pose for a picture. The football was lying on the lawn . . .

Now the Cap'n only had one lung, as was common knowledge, so I couldn't have him running around the lawn or diving to make a save. Instead I

A whole new ball game with Argentine President Carlos Menem. Note Pele's signature on the ball.

suggested that the pair put the ball between their heads, and give each other a big grin. And, on the verandah of the Presidential residence, that's just what they did.

After the meeting, Carlos took me round the back to show me his own pride and joy – his collection of Ferraris (six of them) and top-of-the-range motor-bikes (three Hondas, two Kawasakis). Bob stayed behind in the study.

Afterwards, in the car back to our hotel, his thoughts seemed to be on something else.

At last he said: 'Yes, that black fellow did look useful. Remind me to talk to the Derby manager when we get home.'

The Final Curtain

And now, as Frank Sinatra sang it, the end is near . . .

We all remember – don't we? – exactly where we were on that dreadful day of 22 November in 1963 when President Kennedy fell to an assassin's bullet in Dallas. Similarly, almost everyone I know can remember exactly where they were when they heard of Robert Maxwell's death.

Unlike other figures on the world stage who died after a long illness or sheer old age, the shock waves following the demise of both John Kennedy and Robert Maxwell created massive ripples because they were utterly unexpected, they were violent, and death came ahead of its time.

Certainly every journalist and anyone connected with the media must recall where he or she was on that fateful afternoon of 5 November, 1991.

For myself, I was at my desk in the *People* offices in Holborn, having had a rather good lunch at the Savoy. Actually, it was to celebrate another award – which, I like to think, the Old Man would have appreciated.

No mourning, no negative thoughts, no looking back.

Onward and upward, Mister!

Somebody on the sub-editors' desk shouted across the room. 'Hey, Mike, have you seen this?' A news flash had come up on the screen from the Press Association.

Robert Maxwell missing at sea . . .

As the word spread, every console on every desk throughout the building focused in on the story. After which, for everyone in the organisation and many outside it, life would never be the same again.

I rang the Ninth Floor. Both Kevin and Ian were out, so I left a message with the secretary to say I'd called.

Then I sat back and thought of the last time I had seen the Old Man.

It had been a few days earlier, the evening before he took off for the South of France to pick up the *Lady Ghislaine* for the last voyage of his life. It was in his office and accompanied by the inevitable glass of Dom Perignon. Happy hour, and happy days ahead!

My last memory is of Bob's face staring up at me from the desk as I turned in the doorway. The huge, hypnotic face with its black limpet eyebrows plastered above that shotgun stare that had first paralysed eager young Mr Snapper all those years ago . . .

This time the shotgun wasn't loaded. Cap'n Bob waved me out of the room with a friendly paw and a parting grin, and I closed the door and walked away from the office and from my boss.

I never saw him again.

At the funeral, a weird thing happened. I was positioned right beside the open grave that would shortly become the tomb of Robert Maxwell. The dying sun was spreading its fiery fingers over the minarets and spires of old Jerusalem, turning the sky into a furnace.

Philip Maxwell breaks down on the shoulders of his brothers Ian (left) and Kevin at the funeral.

A huge crowd had gathered on the Mount of Olives for the ceremony which had to be completed, by custom, before sunset. Journalists, TV crews and photographers lined the cemetery walls in silence.

Earlier, Bob's body lay wrapped in the Synagogue like a mummy on a stretcher under a *tallith*, the fringed prayer shawl used by Orthodox Jews on such solemn occcasions, with four candles flickering around it in the autumn dusk. People moved by in a line, shaking hands with Betty Maxwell, with Kevin, Ian, Ghislaine and the rest of the family.

Dignitaries from far and wide had flown in to pay their respects, and the occasion reflected the wide horizons of Bob's life: politicians, bankers, businessmen, scientists, media figures . . .

The Israeli Government was headed by President Herzog and Prime Minister Yitzhak Shamir. The then leader of the opposition Shimon Peres paid tribute to his old friend. 'Bob was a man who looked life in the eye and extracted the utmost from it.' That was for sure.

Because of my closeness to Bob, the family had invited me to take up a post right next to the grave. The other photographers were at least 50 feet away, so they couldn't see what I saw from three feet.

Four pall-bearers brought the stretcher down to the open tomb. One of them jumped down inside. Four other mourners held the *tallith* over the opening, while the bearers tilted the stretcher so that Bob's mummified corpse slid down under the shawl and into the grave.

I ducked under the cloth to witness something quite startling: the lone pall-bearer catching the sliding body and lowering it single-handed into the earth.

That body should have weighed all of 26 stone, and surely wouldn't have been much lighter despite the attentions of the pathologist.

Unless it was Charles Atlas in there, I had just seen something rather odd.

Soon after, Betty Maxwell picked up a handful of sand, and symbolically sprinkled it into the tomb. Earth and stones followed, shovelled in energetically by the grave-diggers who had to get the grave filled in by sunset.

Afterwards, all that was left was a small white board with Bob's name on it to mark the spot.

And now?

Cap'n Bob was the only man I ever met who was an unstoppable force and an immovable object encased in one mountainous body. After more than seven years in the vibrant shadow of that crazy, charismatic Colossus, I knew it would be hard to get back into the real world.

And so it proved.

Believe me, it is not easy to be weaned off a diet of Beluga caviar and Dom

Perignon champagne. Oh, and I almost forgot the lobster claws.

Sometimes I still wonder. Did he fall, or was he pushed?

Now here's something that I also ponder. It is a memory I have of Cap'n Bob and myself, sitting side by side in Gulfstream 2, and the Boss is feeling talkative – as often happened, and when he tended to repeat himself.

But now he is telling me something I had never heard before, or would ever hear again.

'Do you know, Mike, I once jumped off a bridge into a fast-flowing river, just to keep up with the older boys who were all showing off doing it. I was three years old! And I remember going under and thinking I was going to drown. But they fished me out of the water, and I survived. That was the first memory of my life.'

Shivery? Because it would be his last, too. Wouldn't it?

After his death, I read the expert evidence, and like the rest of the world I saw the pictures of the bulbous body laid out on a mortuary slab. I know the conspiracy theories, but I don't honestly believe Bob was murdered by the Mossad, the KGB or the CIA.

I don't think anyone crept up on him in the dead of night and stuck a needle in his neck while he snored away in a drunken stupor.

Nor do I think that he jumped. The one thing of which I feel totally certain is that the Boss would never, ever commit suicide. It simply wasn't in his nature.

I subscribe to the most likely explanation – that the Cap'n toppled overboard on a diet of drink, drugs and despair. He went to the stern to relieve himself – a regular habit – leaned too far over the railing, slipped . . . and that was that.

 You hear all sorts of sounds at sea. If anyone up for'ard had been listening (and why should they?) the far-off splash of Cap'n Bob hitting the water beyond the stern could have been mistaken for just another slap of the waves against the hull of the *Lady G*.

But . . . other images come back to haunt me.

The cosmetic surgeons in South America, with Bob's head bent close, intent, listening. The ease with which a lone grave-digger lifted his end of a 20-stone-plus body . . .

Two and two, making five.

I'm sure it's not so. But one thought keeps nagging at me.

What if . . . ?